THE FINE INSTRUMENT

THE FINE INSTRUMENT

Essays on Katherine Mansfield

edited by
Paulette Michel and Michel Dupuis

Dangaroo  Press

Cover: A detail of the embroidered silk shawl given to
Katherine Mansfield in 1918 by Lady Ottoline Morrell
Photograph: Katherine Mansfield, Brussels, 1906

© Paulette Michel and Michel Dupuis

This book is copyright. Apart from any fair dealing for the purpose of private study, research, criticism or review, as permitted under the Copyright Act, no part may be reproduced by any process without written permission. Enquiries should be made to the publisher.

First published in 1989 by Dangaroo Press
Australia: G.P.O. Box 1209, Sydney, New South Wales, 2001
Denmark: Geding Søvej 21, 8381 Mundelstrup
UK: P.O. Box 186, Coventry CV 4 7H

ISBN 1 871049 61

Contents

ACKNOWLEDGEMENTS	5
INTRODUCTION	7

HOW MANY LIVES

Ian A. GORDON: Katherine Mansfield in the Late Twentieth Century	15
Liselotte GLAGE: Biographies and no End: Katherine Mansfield Criticism in Search of its Subject	28

LIVING AND WRITING

Kate FULLBROOK: Katherine Mansfield: Subjection and Authority	51
Clare HANSON: Katherine Mansfield's Life as a Work of Art	61
Tanya GRENFELL-WILLIAMS: Katherine Mansfield and Time	71
Gillian BODDY: Frau Brechenmacher and Stanley Burnell: Some Background Discussion on the Treatment of the Roles of Men and Women in the Writing of Katherine Mansfield	80

NARRATIVE STRATEGIES

Irène SIMON: Irony in the Short Stories of Katherine Mansfield	97
René GODENNE: Katherine Mansfield's 'Nouvelle-Instant'	107
Andrée-Marie HARMAT: 'Is the master out or in?' or Katherine Mansfield's Twofold Vision of Self	117
Anne HOLDEN RØNNING: Katherine Mansfield, British or New Zealander — The Influence of Setting on Narrative Structure and Theme	126

Claudette SARLET: The Remembered Gardens
Where Writing Wells: An Exploration of Katherine
Mansfield's Work   134

SONGS OF PROTEST

Nelson WATTIE: Katherine Mansfield as a Noble Savage:
The Cry Against Corruption   149

Françoise DEFROMONT: Impossible Mourning   157

Francine TOLRON: Fauna and Flora in Katherine
Mansfield's Short Stories   166

FROM READING TO WRITING

Carole Froude DURIX: Point Counterpoint: Both Sides
of the Broad Road in Katherine Mansfield's 'The Garden
Party' and Witi Ihimaera's 'This Life is Weary'   175

SELECTED BIBLIOGRAPHY   187

NOTES ON CONTRIBUTORS   192

Acknowledgements

We want to express our gratitude to

the Belgian Ministery of Education for their financial contribution to the publication of this volume;

the Belgian Fonds National de la Recherche Scientifique for sponsoring the Liège Katherine Mansfield Centenary Symposium;

the New Zealand Embassy and the British Council in Brussels, the Department of English Literature and the Institut Supérieur des Langues Vivantes of the University of Liège for their generous cooperation.

At the moment of sending the book for print we want to extend our grateful thanks to Hena Maes-Jelinek, Jean-Marie D'Heur, and Cécile Adam, who organized the Symposium with us.

We would also like to thank Gillian Boddy for selecting and providing the illustrations and the Alexander Turnbull library, Wellington for permission to reprint them, our colleagues James Gibbs and Christine Pagnoulle for their help and advice to solve queries, Marc Delrez for reading the proofs and, last but not least, Pierre Michel for his invaluable suggestions and kind assistance in preparing the manuscripts.

Our first and last debts are to our families.

Introduction

MICHEL DUPUIS and PAULETTE MICHEL

Most of the papers collected in this volume were read at the Katherine Mansfield Centenary Symposium held at the University of Liège in October 1988. The aim was to bring together scholars from various critical and geographical horizons, who, in the light of the new material produced in the 70s and 80s, would add to our comprehension of Katherine Mansfield's life and work.

The title of this volume – *The Fine Instrument* – is a quotation from Katherine Mansfield's letters[1] which, we think, epitomizes the many means and strategies she used to express her response to the age in which she lived and her essential convictions about life, and to transmute them into art. Indeed, this collection of papers significantly centers on the analysis both of the nature and of the genesis of the 'strategies' Katherine Mansfield developed -- consciously or not – in her life and in her art. The variety of subjects and of approaches presented here testifies to the new developments in Mansfieldian studies and to her status as a great (woman) writer.

The first section of this volume is devoted to the history of the reception of Katherine Mansfield's work. Ian A. Gordon (New Zealand), a pioneer in Mansfieldian studies, describes in his keynote address the various portraits which emerge from the many biographies of Katherine Mansfield, and concludes that most of them reflect the authors' subjective perception of the woman rather than Katherine Mansfield herself. Liselotte Glage (West Germany) also tackles this question and analyses in detail the biographical approach in search of its object, notably in the most recent works.

The second group of papers testifies to the breakthrough of gender theories in Katherine Mansfield criticism: Kate Fullbrook (Great Britain) accounts for a disjunction between 'a fiction radically committed to an oppositional view of woman and an aesthetic that rejects definition in terms of gender'; she emphasizes the need for the full recognition of women writers as 'architects of consciousness' and 'contributors to ideological change'. Clare Hanson (Great Britain) considers the various pressures and reasons, social, historical, etc., for which Katherine Mansfield transformed her life into a work of art – a process illustrated both in her actual existence and in the self-portrait she constructed in the letters and journals. Tanya Grenfell-Williams (Great Britain) analyses Katherine Mansfield's treatment of time in her fiction in the light of Julia Kristeva's concept of 'women's time'. Gillian Boddy provides biographical background to Katherine Mansfield's exploration of the roles of men and women in her stories.

The third section groups papers which illustrate the technical craftsmanship of her writings. Irène Simon (Belgium) focuses on Katherine Mansfield's use of irony, a subject which has most often been underrated by critics. René Godenne (Belgium), a historian of the French short story, applies his concept of the 'nouvelle-instant' to those of Katherine Mansfield's stories that have been translated into French and have influenced many French 'nouvellistes'. Andrée-Marie Harmat (France) deals with Katherine Mansfield's polyphonic approach to literature and analyses the contrapuntal structure of some stories – an echo of her musical training – as a means to express the twofold dimension of the soul. Anne Holden Rønning (Norway) points to the different ways in which the setting functions in the European and the New Zealand stories. Claudette Sarlet (Belgium) applies a new concept to the study of Katherine Mansfield, namely the psychological locus from which an author's writing springs.

The fourth section voices Katherine Mansfield's songs of protest: Nelson Wattie (West Germany) considers her as an artist and a thinker, and shows that her cry of protest must finally be understood in a broad sense, i.e., against the corruption of the cosmos itself. Françoise Defromont (France) uses psychoanalytical concepts to analyse what she calls 'impossible mourning', and presents this 'impossibility' as a major source of her creative writing. Francine Tolron (France - New Caledonia) considers the ambivalent function of fauna and flora images in the stories as reflecting the difficulty of the human condition.

The fifth and last section is devoted to Carole Froude Durix's paper (France), in which she approaches the phenomenon of intertextuality in a comparison of 'The Garden Party' with 'This Life is Weary', a re-writing of Katherine Mansfield's story by a contemporary Maori writer, Witi Ihimaera.

The work of Katherine Mansfield was long the favourite hunting ground first of the biographers, the hagiographers – eager to know more about her eventful life – then of the 'sensitive' readers eager to analyse the subtle alchemy and the delicate metabolism which produced the short stories. It is now, as manifested in this volume, in the hands of people who want to understand Katherine Mansfield, the woman *and* the writer; people who want to understand how and why they enjoy her writings; how and why her stories also awaken something new in them; how and why the 'instrument' fascinates their souls.

Indeed, critics now have new critical tools which enable them to discover and investigate aspects of the creative process and of the final product to which they simply had no access before. These new critical approaches, combined with the indispensable if more 'traditional' ones, have launched Mansfieldian studies into a new era.

The first and necessary condition for this new development was for the critics to be able to rely on scientific editions of Katherine Mansfield's writings. This is now possible for some of her texts; and all are grateful to those who, in New Zealand, have undertaken the enormous task of editing the manuscripts now in the possession of the Turnbull Library.

Next was it for critics to make a responsible use of all the necessary paratextual information – the biographical elements, the studies of Katherine Mansfield's literary and socio-cultural environment both in New Zealand and in Europe – and to preserve a subtle balance between curiosity and prudence in the analysis of her writings in the light of recent theories (gender, psychoanalytical, etc.). Of course all these partial approaches are 'vulnerable aids', as George Steiner calls them. Yet,

> they matter . . . They enrich the levels of awareness and enjoyment; they generate constrainsts on the complacencies and licence of interpretative anarchy.[2]

Not only do they control our view of the artist and our interpretation of her writings, but they help us to become aware of aspects of her personality and of her work which have so far remained in the dark for lack of the light that would reveal their very existence.

Katherine Mansfield's writings, like all great writers', demand careful reading: it takes patience and attention to appreciate the subtlety of the final construct, the point of the allusions, the lightness of her frames, and the precision of the effects.

But this alone will not yield the full pleasure and knowledge that can be derived from her work. There remain so many things – which are very much there and which may echo differently for each reader – to be discovered: revelations about life, discoveries about the world, about the self, about the other(s), and about death; secret intimations, not explicit messages. Actually Katherine Mansfield's work calls for a kind of reading which aims at comprehending cultural creation in all its aspects – its ethical dimension included, in its two meanings of 'habitation' and 'values' – because writing and reading are indeed a kind of commitment which involves the individual's responsibility, social, cultural, political, etc.; and because the world changes as it is being interpreted.

We hope it will be clear that the contributors to this volume have worked in that direction, and that the sum of the essays will help the reader to get nearer to the core of Katherine Mansfield's texts and to discover and respond to themes which had not yet received the kind of attention that now allows them to tell something more about experience, life and the writing of life, about identity as gender and/or individual character, about technique and the creative process, about the world and about new paths for the spirit. These are questions raised by contemporary philosophers. Katherine Mansfield speaks of them, with Chekhovian discretion, but clearly. And her texts prompt us on to new questionings and to engage in a dialectical dialogue with life and the Mansfieldian text of life. This is, we think, the 'privilege' of great art; this is, we hope, the experience this volume proposes as both a source of pleasure and an incentive to further research.

***

Our editorial policy has been to standardize the references to Katherine Mansfield's texts and to quote from the best editions now available: all the page references to the stories are to Antony Alpers' *The Stories of Katherine Mansfield* (Auckland, Melbourne, Oxford: Oxford University Press, 1984) and are given in the text. The quotations of the letters up to the end of 1919 are from the first two volumes of Vincent O'Sullivan and Margaret Scott's *The Collected Letters of Katherine Mansfield* (Oxford: Clarendon Press, 1984, 1987), while the references to later letters and to the journals are either to John Middleton Murry's *The Letters of Katherine Mansfield* (London: Constable, 1928), *Katherine Mansfield's Letters to John Middleton Murry. 1913-1922* (London: Constable, 1951) and *Journal of Katherine Mansfield* (London: Constable, 1954) or to C.K. Stead's *The Letters and Journals of Katherine Mansfield: A Selection* (Harmondsworth: Penguin, 1977).

NOTES.

1. *The Letters of Katherine Mansfield*, edited by John Middleton Murry, vol. 2 (London: Constable, 1928), p. 202.
2. George Steiner, *Real Presences* (Paris: Vrin, 1988), p. 86.

HOW MANY LIVES

Katherine Mansfield in the Late Twentieth Century

IAN A. GORDON

My title is deliberately vague and gives me plenty of elbow room to move sideways, backwards, forwards and even retreat on occasions.[1]

As an introduction I would like to trace the development of my interest in Katherine Mansfield. I read her short stories as a young graduate back in the mid-thirties before I knew that she was a New Zealander. I enjoyed her enormously: I enjoyed her technique, I enjoyed her attitudes, I enjoyed her portrayal of children; the kind of thing that any unsophisticated young graduate would enjoy, reading Katherine Mansfield, just a few years after she appeared in the periodicals.

When I was translated from a very humble and junior position at the University of Edinburgh to the Chair of English and head of department in the Victoria University of Wellington, I did not know that New Zealand was going to be the country to which I would owe my major allegiance. I did not know that I would later wear the uniform of the New Zealand Army.

I had been in Wellington only a few weeks as a very young, very raw but very busy Professor of English when, leaving the Parliamentary Library, I walked down Molesworth Street (some of you may know it) and looked in the window of a *pâtisserie*, a cake shop. I saw there a tray of delicious looking cream puffs and then I raised my eyes and I saw the name of the shop was Godber. Somewhere at the back of my mind, I thought 'I have seen that name before' and I went back home and picked up my copy of *The Garden Party* and — sure enough — the cream puffs were delivered in the garden party — 'Godber's has come'. Godber's man had arrived. Now, here was the firm of Godber still operating. I had not realized that it was not very long ago, not more than half a generation from the time when Katherine Mansfield had left Wellington and, though she wrote the story in her thirties, she was remembering a period not so very far back when Godber's man did in fact deliver cream puffs. In 1937, Godber made the cream puffs but he had ceased delivery. That is what civilisation does.

From then on I knew I was in Katherine Mansfield country. She was not just words in a book; she was not just a marvellous short story writer who wrote about children in school and all sorts of haunting things that take place in a distant country. She was a writer who was writing about a time and a country that I was actually living in; and from then on I have kept on researching, looking around, identifying the sites, digging up information on Katherine Mansfield. The research still goes on.

I am delighted to be here in the University of Liège tonight and to begin my talk with this note on Katherine Mansfield and me. But I am also going to talk about Katherine Mansfield and other people, because my theme will be the reaction of writers, bibliographers, biographers and critics to Katherine Mansfield.

My first study of Katherine Mansfield — I know the first one mentioned in the bibliographies is my little Longman booklet dated 1954 — has never been reprinted but is worth a mention tonight. During the war years I edited an occasional periodical called *New Zealand New Writing* in which, in 1943, I published my essay entitled 'Katherine Mansfield, New Zealander'. Just think of the impudence of it! Here was I, a young professor from Scotland, not yet carrying a New Zealand passport, daring to write about Katherine Mansfield as a New Zealander.

The truth was I do not think that anyone in New Zealand had noticed how much she was a New Zealander. They knew she had been born in New Zealand, but then she had disappeared in 1908, and had never come back. She had made a great reputation — as a short story writer contributing to the main stream of English literature. Everyone was proud of her, but they did not see her as a New Zealander because they did not see that she spoke with a New Zealand idiom and hardly saw that she was using the New Zealand scene.

I went back the other day to that old essay and I must say I felt I had got some things right which are still right. Katherine Mansfield is essentially a New Zealander. She writes about Europe, she writes about things that are not New Zealand, but the important stories are enshrined in a New Zealand setting and also (something that has not yet been fully worked out by any researcher) in New Zealand idiom.

Not all the stories that you read in the readily available texts are precisely as Katherine Mansfield wrote them. I mention only one example. One of her very early stories, written when she was at school in Queen's College in London, has a girl saying of the French master that perhaps he 'will shout us a threepenny vanilla'. A threepenny vanilla is, of course, an icecream. Middleton Murry editing this story, which he did after Katherine Mansfield was dead, either did not know or did not want to know what the word 'shout' meant. He deleted it and printed 'give'. The New Zealanders present will know that 'shout' equals the English colloquial form 'treat'. When you buy someone a drink in a pub in New Zealand, you shout them a drink; you do not give them a drink, you shout them.

This is something that has not been picked up very often by readers of Katherine Mansfield, particularly readers in Continental Europe, the considerable amount of New Zealand colloquial idiom which is interspersed through her stories and of course, to an even greater extent, in her letters. She is a New Zealander; she is a New Zealander because of her material; she is a New Zealander because of her use of language.

She is much more than that. Here, towards the end of the 20th century, she is an industry, in this her centenary year, almost as busy as the Shakespeare industry; books and articles and reprints pour out. I had the curious experience two months ago, once it was confirmed that I was coming to Liège, of deciding to re-read every book and most of the articles that have been written on Katherine Manfield. It was quite an exercise I can assure you, and I emerged from it a bit shaken by the experience.

There are, in a sense, two Katherine Mansfields. There is Katherine Mansfield the heroine of a whole series of biographical studies and there is Katherine Mansfield the writer.

I begin with Katherine Mansfield the person. There have been many Katherine Mansfields and each has depended on who is painting the picture. The first picture of all was the biography of Katherine Mansfield done by Ruth Mantz, a young American scholar who visited New Zealand and gossiped to some of the people who had known her, then went to England and met Middleton Murry. Middleton Murry apparently co-operated because it is clear from internal evidence he showed Ruth Mantz the manuscript of the journal that I edited as *The Urewera Notebook*. The Mantz life is known in its French translation as *La jeunesse de Katherine Mansfield*. It is just that.

That was all there was when I started working on Katherine

Mansfield. I did not believe everything but it was in print and what is in print has a certain degree of authority. It was not till years later that I realized that a great deal of it is nonsense.

The Katherine Mansfield of Ruth Mantz is the first Katherine Mansfield: the rebellious adolescent, the young girl who grew up in New Zealand, who was sent to a finishing school in Queen's College in Harley Street in London, and who went back and grumbled and fought with her family and threw tantrums and finally persuaded the Beauchamp family to send her grudgingly back to New Zealand. I call the Mantz version the rebellious adolescent. It is not true; but there it was in print.

The next Katherine Mansfield, of course, is Middleton Murry's Katherine Mansfield. She died in 1923; by that time two of her volumes were in print. Middleton Murry produced two more volumes of short stories; he produced two volumes of letters; he produced an edition of the *Journal* and the *Journal* became a classic because of the extraordinary writing of the woman who wrote the words.

As I have pointed out in another context, she did not write a journal at all; she simply kept a heap of notes, a handful of diaries (thinly entered up), and a mass of flying bits of paper. Middleton Murry put these together, not always accurately, and sometimes cheated by putting two bits of paper together as if they were continuous pieces of prose although there is no evidence that they were written on the same day or even in the same year. It is an extraordinary mixture but it is a remarkable piece of editorial manipulation.

The manipulation went on for years but the Katherine Mansfield of Middleton Murry was the Katherine Mansfield of a man who — but I am not going into the relationship between Middleton Murry and Katherine Mansfield; I am concerned only with the posthumous Katherine Mansfield that Middleton Murry produced. Again, it was not the real thing. She is a saint; she is a nebulous, ghostly, wraith-like creature who can do no wrong, she is all for purity — and of course a marvellous writer too. The saint legend kept on going and going and for a number of years it impressed itself on the French imagination. The first French Katherine Mansfield is Katherine Mansfield the saint.

The next Katherine Mansfield was Sylvia Berkman's; of all the books written on Katherine Mansfield, I still find myself going back again and again to that magnificent American scholar. Sylvia Berkman got some things wrong; she had no option; she had no option because she was basing her material on the Mantz life: the rebellious adolescent. 'For months she agonized' — I am paraphrasing but that is pretty well what Sylvia Berkman says, picking it up from Ruth Mantz. But apart from that I found her portrait extremely accurate and certainly on the bibliographical and the critical sides, it is still one of the best books on Katherine Mansfield. It was produced back in the 1950s.

The next Katherine Mansfield is the production of what I call Alpers Mark I. Antony Alpers (1953 in America, 1954 in England), produced the first massive biography. He was a young journalist who had done extremely good work in New Zealand. He produced Mark I in 1954 and I was greatly impressed by the power of investigative journalism of this young man. He had really dug into the kind of thing that good investigative journalists did.

We all knew back in the thirties and the forties that Katherine Mansfield married a man called George Bowden — you know the rest of the story — and then Bowden just disappeared from the scene. What did Alpers do? He found Bowden; he tracked him down and got the story of what really happened; Bowden's written account is now in the Turnbull Library in Wellington. Nobody had bothered looking for Bowden; he was just a lost husband — lost en route. I pay tribute to that investigative ability of Antony Alpers.

But alas he made one major mistake in the 1954 volume partly because — and one must be fair to him — because the material was simply not available. The manuscripts we now have in the Turnbull Library, the great mass of papers and correspondence, were not in public hands. Middleton Murry was jealously guarding all the shreds and pieces, hugging them to his bosom, manipulating them for his version. Alpers had no opportunity of seeing the documentation which is now possible for scholars to examine.

Alpers was led into one major error. He has since largely retracted in his later Mark II biography but unfortunately it is still leaving a mark on the life and works of Katherine Mansfield as seen by many critics. I am talking about her relationship with Harold Beauchamp, her father. Alpers, in his first 1954 volume, has an appendix called 'Money Matters'. He starts off by quoting an unknown person. This is an old journalistic ploy, guarding one's sources. Scholarship should never guard sources. An unknown person, 'a friend in London who said that...' I do not trust the evidence of 'a friend in London who said that...'; I like to know what precisely was said, what the name of the friend was, and how reliable the date and the documentation are. The friend in London said that Katherine Mansfield did not get on with her father because her father was the richest man in New Zealand and the meanest.

I think the friend was L.M., Ida Baker, and I do not trust a word that Ida Baker says or writes. She came out with her own memoirs, ghosted by somebody else, when she was a very old lady: it is therefore necessary to approach with care that very complex Ida Baker/Katherine Mansfield situation. L.M. was a friend, a supporter and an utter bugbear to poor K.M. who depended on her but, sometimes, hated her guts. When they were together in the South of France in 1918, L.M.'s extravagance drove K.M. furious; L.M. could not speak French, she could not handle French currency, she was always being cheated at the market and Katherine Mansfield 'cried poverty' — to L.M., but to nobody else. If you have read that appendix 'Money Matters', forget it. It is nonsense.

Harold Beauchamp supported Katherine Mansfield from the day she was born to the day she died, and supported her in very adequate amounts. You probably know the general shape of the story, but what very few people do is to wind the time clock backwards and think of the value of money. In the early years of this century, we all know that Katherine Mansfield came to London in 1908 on an allowance of two pounds a week and everyone exclaims 'Two pounds a week?' How could anyone send a daughter to England on two pounds a week? It is monstrous!'.

But, if you think of the cost of living and what two pounds a week in London bought in 1908, the situation is very different. I had a yarn with our Professor of Economic History a few weeks ago. What factor would he apply to two pounds a week in 1908 to equate it to today's value in present-day London? His rough estimate was of the order of 75 to 100.

Two pounds a week was in 1908 the wage of a skilled mechanic, who was supporting a wife and two children. He would not have any spare money at the end of the week but he could survive. Katherine Mansfield had that amount of money for herself.

When Middleton Murry met her first, he rushed out and bought a copy of her *In a German Pension*. It cost him two shillings, brand new. Think of that in terms of two pounds a week. Take the price of a new novel in London and multiply that by twenty and you begin to get a quite different picture of the situation. When Katherine Mansfield arrived in London she lived in a very pleasant hostel for music students, paying 25 shillings a week for board and lodgings. That gave her all her meals, seven days a week, a room with a carpet and furnishing, heating, which in London is important, a maid bringing up the coal. That accounted for five-eighths of her allowance. The other fifteen shillings she had for spending money.

She was not badly off. If you look at the first volume of her letters in the magnificent new edition, you will find that from time to time she comes home in a hansom cab. How many students these days in London can afford to come home in a taxi, which is the equivalent? Theatre — the cheaper seats in a theatre in London in 1908 were sixpence. You try and get a seat in the National Theatre today under seven pounds and you would be lucky. So there is the equation — sixpence equals seven pounds.

My impression is that so far as buying power goes, Katherine Mansfield in her first few years was provided by her family with the kind of money that, at the present day, a young graduate teacher in Britain or a young assistant in his or her first job in university would be earning. That is what the equation produces, an income of about five to six thousand pounds a year. I know it sounds incredible, but these are the facts of the case.

The income continued. It was stepped up a few years later and Katherine Mansfield wrote what one biographer has called a pathetically grateful letter. Somebody else calls it a dutiful letter. Well, I have read the letter carefully and to me it reads like a nice letter, 'thanks very much father for raising my allowance'. I do not see anything pathetic about it. I do not see anything humble or submissive about it; it is just a nice-thank-you letter.

The income continued to be stepped up. Alpers even in Mark II continues to regard Harold Beauchamp as suspect. Yet, in 1919, Beauchamp decided to fix up all his daughters with a decent allowance. The documents are in the Turnbull Library; there is no need to question them; they can be authenticated by cross-references elsewhere. There were four girls: Vera, Chaddie, Jeanne, the youngest, and Katherine. He settled shares on Vera which produced two hundred pounds a year. He settled shares on Chaddie which produced two hundred pounds a year. He settled an income, paid differently, on the youngest : two hundred pounds a year.

On Katherine, the black sheep, the escapee, the legendary rebellious daughter: *three hundred pounds* a year. In other words, he settled on her 50% more than he settled on the other girls. Later on, he gradually brought all the girls up to equal amounts. This gives the complete lie to the earlier errors of Alpers Mark I; it also invalidates some of the things that he says in his revised version. He has gone back on quite a few of the allegations he made earlier, but Mark II still leaves a nasty taste. Somewhere in the background there still lurks wealthy Harold Beauchamp, blind to a starving artist daughter.

This is the third Katherine. You get Katherine Mansfield, the rebellious adolescent. You get Katherine Mansfield the saint. And then you get Katherine Mansfield, the starving artist with the wicked banker somewhere back in the colonies. What worries me is that this last portrait, although the documents show that it is entirely wrong, still persists and continues to affect other biographies, including one that came out only a few months ago.

Money does matter, but we must be careful in our assessments. The so-called definitive edition of Katherine Mansfield's short stories (which is anything but definitive) has one section in the introduction where there is a discussion of the small group of stories she wrote for *The Sphere*, for which Clement Shorter paid her a fee. Clement Shorter, we are told, 'flung his money-bags at the dying Katherine Mansfield'. This is claptrap, journalism at its worst. We know now in retrospect that she was dying but Clement Shorter did not know. He simply offered her a commercial proposition.

If you look very carefully at her correspondence you will find that Katherine Mansfield was very proud that she could write on different levels. 'If you shake me,' she said to Middleton Murry on one occasion, 'you will find that money will fall out', or words to that effect. In other words, 'I can write for money and I know I can write for money', and she talks in one of her letters of the kind of writing one does for cash and the kind of writing that she did not do for cash. She made a distinction between her serious stories and her light stories, the latter available for cash.

The portraits increase in number. We have had three Katherine Mansfields. There is a fourth and a fifth and a sixth emerging almost every day. There is Katherine Mansfield the feminist; I do not intend to touch that topic. You ladies can decide whether she is a feminist or not but she is of course a woman; she is a woman writer so far as I am concerned. So what? To me she is one of the great writers of the twentieth century. The fact that she is female is a bonus but it does not really explain her skill.

Before I left Wellington I noticed that the local sorority of the lesbians association were meeting in my university to discuss 'the real Katherine Mansfield', evidently a sister-figure. Naturally, I was not invited to the session and may never know the outcome.

I think we all tend to see in Katherine Mansfield what we want to see. Middleton Murry, shocked at her death and reading over these dreadful letters she sent from the South of France, wanted a dear departed saint. He created one. Ruth Mantz wanted a story of a young girl growing up. Antony Alpers wanted a dramatic story with plenty of journalistic blacks and whites. I was amused some years ago when I produced my volume called *Undiscovered Country* to find one of the reviewers say that Professor Gordon took altogether a too paternal view of Katherine Mansfield. Perhaps I do see in her a clever daughter. We have all got to watch our own biases.

The most recent tendency is towards the sensational. The very titles are a give-away: in France, M. Pierson-Pierard's *La vie passionnée de Katherine Mansfield*, in England C. Tomalin's *Katherine Mansfield. A Secret Life*.[2] I found the latter book most unsatisfactory. It is studded with factual errors in the early sections, the author writing of a New Zealand writer without having visited New Zealand and without any understanding of her distinctively New Zealand linguistic usages; and neither Professor O'Sullivan, the editor of the standard edition of the letters, nor I know of a scrap of evidence to substantiate the Tomalin account of the 'blackmail' incident; it is pure fantasy.

I turn back with some relief to the year 1957. Middleton Murry left in his will an instruction that the originals of Katherine Mansfield's letters to him should be offered to the British Museum for a thousand pounds sterling and, in the event of the British Museum not wishing to take up the purchase, they should be offered for the same amount to the Turnbull Library in Wellington. I was then a committee member of the Friends of the Turnbull Library and we called a meeting with the Librarian. We decided to see either the P.M. or the Minister of Finance and there was no problem about money.

We then wrote to the British Museum and told them about the contents of the will and said 'of course you have not got a thousand pounds' and the British Museum wrote back and said 'of course we have not got a thousand pounds; we could not afford a thousand pounds for the letters'. In other words the B.M., like gentlemen, stepped back and the Turnbull Library acquired the letters. We also, in the same year, discovered that Sothebys were offering an enormous pile of Katherine Mansfield papers and again we got government support for the purchase. The Deputy High Commissioner in London bid at the auction and the papers arrived in Wellington.

I was the first person, apart from the Librarian, in New Zealand to look over the Katherine Mansfield documents and my eyes just popped. Here were her diaries; here were drafts of stories; here were letters; here were notebooks; here was all the evidence of a writer in her workshop; a writer who was a dedicated worker, not a nonsense adolescent, not a grieving, impoverished artist, but a real woman, sitting at her desk and getting down to the job of work. And this to me is the real Katherine Mansfield; the woman who really gets down to a job of work. She is the most dedicated professional I think I have ever come across in the world of writing. What matters to her is not money, not reputation, although she wants these in modest amounts, but work, work, work.

Even as schoolgirl she writes in one of her letters 'I must get down to work'. In one of her notebooks she writes about her mother 'the one thing she doesn't know anything about is work'. She is not talking about housework. She is not talking about organizing the cooking or the baking or running the servants. She is talking about sheer professionalism. Katherine Mansfield is, from tip to toe, a professional and she is dedicated to the idea that you have to work at your métier; that is one of the reasons (though only one of the reasons) why she is so effective.

I went over this jumble of notebooks and loose sheets of paper (at that stage unsorted and uncatalogued) and I realized this was the raw material from which Middleton Murry had quarried the *Journal* and from which he quarried the later 1954 'definitive' edition. It is no more definitive than the Apocrypha.

I can assure you the 1954 'definitive' edition of the *Journal* is a botched job. I took my own copy to the Turnbull Library and spent months comparing it sheet by sheet and page by page with the papers that Middleton Murry transcribed. I have brought it with me. Let me just open it at one page. It is covered with pencil corrections: my transcriptions from Katherine Mansfield manuscripts which differ from the transcriptions of Middleton Murry.

In my edition of the *Urewera Notebook*, I had the same problem. When I was editing it, I found that this was a notebook which Katherine Mansfield had written in 1907, which she carried with her to England in 1908, and which had remained with her all her life. When Middleton Murry came across it after her death he tried to transcribe it for the 1954 *Journal*. The handwriting is bad, and he was faced with the diary of a girl he did not know, Katherine Mansfield aged eighteen, operating in a country he had never been in, and working in a language (some of it Maori) that he could not understand.

He got it completely and disastrously wrong. He even got it so wrong that he led Ruth Mantz astray. One of the key misreadings (which she adopted in her 1933 *Life*) occurs when Katherine Mansfield visits Rotorua. Murry printed the passage in 1954 as 'Rotarua — that little Hell'. From this 'little Hell' sprang the myth of the disgruntled adolescent. What Katherine Mansfield wrote was 'that little Hill', referring to an enjoyable excursion on the way to Rotorua.

I have been working among these papers for years. I do not think I shall be publishing any more editions from them. Margaret Scott, who transcribed the letters which Professor O'Sullivan has annotated, is working on a full edition. Fortunately, a team of younger scholars is now in the game.

This brings me within sight of my conclusion. If any of you are working on Katherine Mansfield I think my advice is 'Beware'. Be very cautious about working on her biographical material unless you are absolutely certain that your feet are on solid ground. There has been built up over the years a whole pyramid of misconceptions. You get the mistakes, some deliberate, some unconscious, of Ruth Mantz and Middleton Murry. You get the mistakes, most of them misapprehensions, of Alpers Mark I. You get the continuous infiltration of these various misinterpretations into later work. You get the mistranscriptions of the *Journal* material. All of this is cumulative and if you come in at the top of the pile you are building on a very unsure foundation.

Fortunately, a new platform is being built. The letters are at last appearing in an accurate edition. Margaret Scott has spent years on the transcriptions, and her work is being supplemented by the annotation and editing of Professor O'Sullivan. We are now on a new level of Katherine Mansfield scholarship, and I am glad that the new level is being produced in New Zealand. It is not until you get real New Zealand scholars, who know their New Zealand and the New Zealand vocabulary, who know the New Zealand ambience and landscape as well as the European side of Katherine Mansfield, that such an edition is possible. We are laying a solid foundation on which further Katherine Mansfield studies can be firmly based.

There is still much to do. It is not my brief tonight to speak of Katherine Mansfield criticism. There is a great deal of it; and yet we await a really penetrating book on Katherine Mansfield as a short story writer. I do not mean a historical, chronological, survey of her writing from 'The Education of Audrey' to 'The Fly'. I am talking of a real analysis of the big stories : 'At the Bay', 'The Daughters of the Late Colonel', 'Prelude' and so on. 'The "Prelude" method — it just unfolds and opens' — that is one of the key indicators. If you work carefully through her letters, particularly those to Middleton Murry's brother and to Brett, and the critical remarks she drops from time to time, I think there are sufficient clues for one to work out what she was striving at; how she came to the great secret, the great secret of re-creating the short story; cutting away the nonsense; sloughing away the 'he said, she said, he thought, she thought' clutter; getting right down to that immediacy of impact which is the hallmark of her best work.

The editing of the letters should be complete in a few more years. It may take longer to edit the mass of papers in the Turnbull Library. I hope it will not be too long. There are still discoveries to be made. Some will surprise you. That Carco affair in 1915 — it is well documented in her diary of that year, although Murry's selective editing of it in the 1954 *Journal* leaves much obscure. Murry notes that after the affair she 'returned disillusioned to England'. I do not think that Katherine Mansfield had any illusions on what she was about. There is strong evidence in the 1915 diary that the Carco episode was yet another of her attempts to gain first-hand experience: she could write only about what she *knew*.

Katherine Mansfield was utterly ruthless in her search for 'experience'. Even as a schoolgirl in Wellington she confided in her notebook, concerning a young man with whom she had a mild flirtation, 'I used him only for copy'. Carco was another piece of copy. It does not make Katherine Mansfield a very nice person, but a woman dedicated as she was to her work has no time to be a nice person.

I had better pause, before I destroy any more of your illusions. Katherine Mansfield is one of my heroines. I hope she remains one of yours.

NOTES

1. This keynote address was delivered extempore on 14 October 1988 at the University of Liège on the occasion of the Katherine Mansfield centenary conference. It was recorded on tape and the text is edited from a transcription. Apart from correcting some oral slips and eliminating asides, I have left the text in the spoken register in which it was delivered. (I.A.G.)

2. M. Pierson-Pierard, *La vie passionnée de Katherine Mansfield* (Bruxelles: Labor-Nathan, 1979); C. Tomalin, *Katherine Mansfield. A Secret Life* (London: Viking, 1987).

Biographies and no End: Katherine Mansfield Criticism in Search of its Subject

LISELOTTE GLAGE

'Katherine Mansfield was born a century ago and died in 1923, but there is still something tantalizing about the "faint ghost with the steady eyes, the mocking lips and, at the end, the wreath set on her hair."' These are the opening words in Claire Tomalin's *Katherine Mansfield. A Secret Life*.[1] A new biography to celebrate the centenary in 1988? The 'definitive critical biography' that Elizabeth Webby had been hoping for since 1982?[2]

While Webby expected future biographies, after Alpers' work[3], 'to capture the elusive real Mansfield' (p. 242), Tomalin's aim is to write a historical biography. On the basis of the material that has been appearing over the last decade, she wants to reassess some of the old assumptions and shed new light on some of Katherine Mansfield's relationships — with Murry, of course; with Lawrence and Woolf; and with Sobieniowski. Also, Tomalin's perspective is different from that of her male predecessors. She looks at Katherine Mansfield with the sympathy of a woman, and shares her predicament: 'taking a traditional female role, but also seeking male privileges' (p. 2) could provide her with a view that is less obstructed by gender prejudices. Yet this book, meant to come out in the 70s and published at the end of the 80s, offers a historical biography at a time when 'post-histoire' and its corollary questionings of modernism and post-modernism are ruffling even academic bosoms. We are offered a woman's *Life* that shows sympathetic female bonding but hardly any theoretical feminist groundwork at a time when post-feminism is being ushered in. However, I do not want to suggest that this book is superannuated or superfluous. On the contrary: not only is it excellent reading (in fact the only readable Katherine Mansfield biography), but it also poses a host of new questions.

After all, literary history cannot boast of very many similar cases. Only 65 years after the death of a writer — of one, moreover, with a 'modest body of work'[4] — her memorial library is furnished with an impressive body of biographical work:[5] in Great Britain and the US alone there are now seven biographies; one biography, one biographie romancée, a poem and two films in New Zealand; four biographies, an ode, a play and a novel in France; one biography and one novel in W. Germany; a novel in Austria; a biographical tale in Italy. To this we have to add countless articles in journals, and chapters in books, that approach interpretation through biography. However, there is no complete critical edition of Katherine Mansfield's stories, and we have to thank Alpers for having at least begun that task.[6]

No doubt Alpers' second biography was a landmark in Katherine Mansfield research. Even so he himself felt uneasy: 'Having committed biography twice I sometimes wonder, after that, whether it ought to be allowed.'[7] He qualifies his own position:

> Not the knowledge of the participants in the story, but the customs of the time in which the teller of it lives, the currently accepted expectations of biography, will play a shaping part. They have greatly changed, between 1950 and 1980. The construct which results may be seen as true, but only for its time. Such a thing as a 'definitive biography' does not exist. Because of the changes in the view we take, it will always be changing. (p. 370b)

This qualification, however, does not transcend the traditional view of biography but, rather, encourages its continuation. Dennis Mceldowney, in his 1985 review article, offers quite a different view:

> The multiplication of interpretations becomes an aspect of the biography itself. No one writes meta-biography, as it were, with the deliberate intention of casting doubt on the possibilities of biography itself. People write new biographies because they believe they have a firmer grasp on the truth of the matter than those who have written before. . . . Yet the more the trick is repeated the more the reader's confidence must be undermined in the ability to find and tell all the truth, and even in there being a final truth to find.[8]

Meta-biography should indeed, I think, be the main aim in Katherine Mansfield research, not only in questions of genuine historical interest, but also in another sense.

More than 25 years have passed since Booth replaced the real by the implied author, and 10 years since Barthes tolled the death-knell of the author. Structuralists and post-structuralists alike have confirmed and reconfirmed processes of signification beyond the 'merely' personal. And yet we still seem to be yearning for what

Octavio Paz at one time called the secret subject of modernity: true presence. In 1978 Magalaner demanded that after so many years of new critical analyses we should return to the writer: 'If only as a corrective, perhaps the time has come to put Katherine Mansfield back into her stories.'9 As a matter of fact, Katherine Mansfield critics had never ceased searching for the 'traces of her "Self"' (Magalaner) or for the 'elusive real Mansfield'. In 1931 Cox had taken Katherine Mansfield as a witness for the close connection between her life and work: 'You see — to me, life and work are two things indivisible. It's only by being true to life that I can be true to art.'10 And as late as 1983 Hankin reads Katherine Mansfield's texts as confessional stories, which, in turn, justifies her own approach of text and biography as mutually informing components of one body. But then, have we not learned to mistrust a writer's own self-interpretation? Small wonder that Clare Hanson insists on her own 'shifting attention away from the attractive personality . . . back to the writing.'11

Latent or manifest, the main question in Katherine Mansfield criticism is that concerning the subject and its self. The answers found are as ambivalent as they are unanimous. This should hardly surprise us if we take into consideration what Alpers and Mceldowney have been suggesting: literary criticism and its discourse on texts and their history is, at one and the same time, discourse on literary critics, their history, their script, their self. Varied as this discourse may be, it yet derives from one source, the logical principle of identity inscribed in the symbolical order of white, male, Western culture. The various biographical attempts appear to me as iconographies of the female subject-as-object, all relying on the same system of representation: that of the subject as free, unified, centred, autonomous; in other words: male.

***

Preceding the critics' discourse, but tied up with it at a very early stage, comes Katherine Mansfield's own discourse, the discourse of a woman continually designing new roles, new images of and for herself, putting on new guises like new dresses: for whom 'impersonation' constitutes the main pleasure of writing;12 and who goes on asking, almost to the end, where to find her own, 'true', self.

> True to oneself! which self? Which of my many — well really, that's what it looks like coming to — hundreds of selves? . . . there are signs that we are intent as never before on trying to puzzle out, to live by, our own particular self . . . free, disentangled, single. Is it not possible that the rage for confession, autobiography, especially for memories of earliest childhood, is explained by our persistent yet mysterious belief in a self which is continuous and permanent . . . This is the moment which, after all, we live for — the moment of direct feeling when we are most ourselves and least personal.[13]

This is probably one of the passages quoted most frequently whenever readers were looking for the 'elusive real Mansfield'. Critics have only too willingly adopted Katherine Mansfield's words, have interpreted them as the pursuit of the authentic, the undivided, the unified self, and have attempted to establish that self. Katherine Mansfield, however, knew that 'puzzling out' her 'own particular self' was to remain a desire to be gratified only momentarily and embracing gain and loss. I think that Katherine Mansfield is here describing what we, today, understand as the process of deconstruction of the bourgeois subject, more particularly the problems of the construction of the female subject. I shall return to this 'gendered vision' later.

There are two more aspects in Katherine Mansfield's urge for self-expression that had a strong impact on criticism. One is her own aggressiveness in dramatizing her pursuit. This dramatization, the avowed programme of trying on new roles, was something which, for a long time, remained hidden from her readers as well as her critics. Wagenknecht was one of the very few who became aware at an early stage (1928) not only of her 'profound sincerity' but also of 'her wisdom . . . her terrifying power to read bare the human soul'.[14]

The publication of the *Journal* in 1927 and the *Letters* in 1928 in Murry's polished version allowed the imagination free play, if only in one direction. Murry's expurgations — most notably those of the letters of the later years with their increasing pressure through physical illness, mental anguish and 'religious dilemma'[15] — were bound to produce the image of the lonely, loving, suffering, tormented soul in a gracefully frail (childlike!) body. It has been asked whether this image did not perhaps conform to one of Katherine Mansfield's own projections of herself. Tomalin, commenting on Katherine Mansfield's will of 1922, in which she asks Murry to destroy all letters and papers he did not want to use, concludes quite rightly that she might have done so herself.[16]

The second aspect that seems important to me is this. In a letter of March 1920, Katherine Mansfield writes: 'It is a great strain to live away from one's own tribe, with people who, however dear they are, are not ARTISTS. These people's minds are about 1894 — not a day later.' What, for Katherine Mansfield, is a token not only of her existence as an artist, but also of her very modernity, results in something very different in literary criticism. In 1940, Whitridge comments on this passage:

> The underlying assumption so characteristic of the romantic that artists are a race apart, free from obligations that fetter the rest of humanity, explains the brilliance, the waywardness, and the pathos of her career.'[17]

In subsuming her under 'the romantic' and thus 'explaining' the specificity of her art, Whitridge not only robs Katherine Mansfield of her own sense of historicity, but also paves the way for an image of Katherine Mansfield that links itself neatly to that of the great sufferer. For decades to come, Katherine Mansfield's name would evoke notions of the tragic genius on the margins of society, of fragility, purity, illness and early death. These notions also provided the key to an understanding of her texts, not only while the cult lasted, and not only in France, and they were easily amalgamated into the image of greatness and heroism.[18]

The image cultivated by Murry and gladly accepted by readers and critics received nasty scratches when *Letters* and *Journal,* far less bowdlerized than before, and Alpers' first biography appeared in the 50s. The wider public found itself confronted with a Katherine Mansfield who was anything but fragile, pure, and loving. Instead, she was discovered to have consisted of real flesh and blood, of hate, lies, and bisexuality. In France, people were unprepared for the shock, and only few, like Francois Mauriac, were prepared to acknowledge it.[19] In England, rumours had been spreading for some time. Now, an illusion of perfection was broken. The subject/object, which had lent itself to being moulded to such perfection, seemed to be disappearing. Her identity had to be recaptured, defined and re-formed.

***

There was no lack of material for such a re-definition. Alpers had to tread carefully, because Murry continued making his influence felt; also, quite a few of Katherine Mansfield's contemporaries were still alive and their private freedom had to be protected. Some of Alpers' findings, however, were new even to Murry.

Re-definition, or re-construction, began via the interpretation of the texts.[20] Soon, Katherine Mansfield research entered the stage of seriously collecting and securing material and sources, in particular the early, unpublished texts. After Murry's death in 1957, free access was finally possible to all the letters, notes and journals. In the following 20 years another mine was opened with, for example, the release of Virginia Woolf's diaries. In 1971 Ida Baker's *Katherine Mansfield: The Memories of L.M.* was issued. The time was ripe for a new round of biographical investigation, by a new generation with, perhaps, a new approach.

I shall concentrate on Meyers, Alpers (1980) and Tomalin, i.e., on the three biographies written in English, which seem to have been most influential and which belong to the more strictly academic kind of presentation (I am including Tomalin, although she regards herself as non-academic). However, there are some other biographies which, in West Germany at least, claim a large audience of dilettanti who, when they read the books by Schwendimann, Citati or Crone, find themselves confronted with a Katherine Mansfield of and for lovers.

In these 'lives' there is little or no attempt at veiling the incomprehensible, the unconventional, even the malignant in Katherine Mansfield. But the way in which her personality is developed is such that it allows, even invites, identification and complicity with the suffering, female, artist, with the genius in the worst sense of 'romantic' otherworldliness. These biographies take their readers back to the époque of the cult and its aura of glowing, admirable strangeness.

With Schwendimann (1967), this does not come as a surprise. His life-and-letters approach shows his affiliation with the type of German *Geistesgeschichte*, which still held its ground for many years after the Second World War. He has read Alpers (1953) and Berkman, but his real debt is to Mantz/Murry, Marcel and Merlin.

In the introduction to her edition of the *Critical Writings*, Hanson points out the pitfalls of a romanticizing attitude:

> it has been suggested that her finest critical insights came in an impromptu fashion, and were dashed off in moments of inspiration in letters and journals. This rather romantic view both fosters and depends on an over-emphasis on the immediately accessible 'personality' of the author, which, it is supposed, is reflected in all her writings. (p. 2)

This, precisely, is what we are getting from Schwendimann. We are back with the

> spontaneity of Katherine Mansfield's art . . . it is this purifying process which explains most readily the simplicity with which Katherine Mansfield was able to represent some of the complexest and least tangible states of emotion. This is no mere matter of technique, but the result of her own spiritual purification and reformation towards a state of crystalline transparency. This state was her ultimate goal, for which she fought, suffered, prayed, and finally, sacrificed her life. (pp. 249-250, my translation)

While the prayer for crystal clearness is, of course, Katherine Mansfield's own, Schwendimann's characterization contributes to almost refining away the subject. The French philosopher Gabriel Marcel, too, had stood in awe of this process of spiritual cleansing (ascese), when he read Katherine Mansfield's letter to Brett dated 2 April 1922.[21]

Such spiritual cleansing will carry before it any contradiction, any jarring doubt, the incomprehensibly strange is re-integrated into the human fold. 'Katherine Mansfield, as a friend once said, had a greater talent than anybody he had ever known or read about, to be purely and simply human.'[22] This humanity of Katherine Mansfield has, via the process of sublimation, been emptied of her desire for fulness and fulfilment. Where Katherine Mansfield was regretting a lack, her critics (re)instituted 'unité intérieure'.

With Citati, worse is to come. His biographical tale (1980) is a strange amalgam of (unacknowledged) quotes from Katherine Mansfield's texts and awed admiration of the dainty, even the ineffable.[23]

The metaphors used by the biographers — a crystal in Schwendimann, oriental pottery in Citati — indicate that reification of the female subject could hardly be pushed any further.[24] The psychoanalytic vocabulary Citati introduces seems to promise a new approach and with it a possibly less restricted notion of subject-positions. He talks about narcissism (p. 10), identity unattained (p. 13) and infantile fixation (p. 53), about hysteria as a source of inspiration (p. 12) and of the mise-en-scène of the drama of her soul (p. 51). Only too soon do we discover that these concepts hold the status of metaphors, the subject disappears behind the image. Schwendimann allowed his Katherine Mansfield at least something like her own shape and stature. At the end of Citati's *Vita breve*, the butterfly-as-Chinese-doll image indicates once again the dehumanization through adoration, an adoration which, I cannot help feeling, has a touch of necrophilia about it.

In a recent novel by the East-German writer Christa Moog, one of the characters begs the first-person narrator not to elevate Katherine Mansfield to sainthood. This is what Citati and, in his way, Schwendimann do. They have polished away any tarnishing spots, re-unified the divided self and lifted it (not her, because in their books the woman has all but ceased to exist) onto a pedestal. It remains to be seen how Katherine Mansfield's more professional biographers deal with the ambiguity of 'femme fatale/femme fragile' — if these are at all valid notions.

Before doing this, I should like to look briefly at one last book. Under the stress of her medical studies Nora Crone used to escape to the Literary Section, where she discovered Lawrence, Murry and Katherine Mansfield and was attracted by the 'bird of paradise from a southern ocean' (p. 7). If such a thing is possible, Crone is even more in sympathy with Katherine Mansfield than is Citati, and entirely adopts the point of view of her heroine, this 'impulsive, impetuous, passionate little being!' (p. 70). Citati's 'femme fragile' is now reduced to an almost childlike figure. This is probably one reason why Crone will, now and again, gloss things over or, if speak she must, do so with almost bashful discretion. 'Sorapure did the inestimable service to Katherine of finally diagnosing the cause of the vicious "rheumatism"'(p. 231). If we had not known, as we have done for about thirty years now, what this 'cause' was, this book would not tell us anything about it (although Crone, the physician, will tell us the most astonishing things about 'normal' feelings of pregnant women). One of the inestimable services Alpers and Tomalin did to Katherine Mansfield was to show that precision of biographical detail need not be coarse.

The reformed, the unworldly, the child-woman: these are notions of femininity which were not buried with the Victorian age and which we find inscribed into the life of a woman who had insisted on not living 'about 1894'. A woman, moreover, who was not unique in her time but, like other women of that time — Jean Rhys, Djuna Barnes, Gertrude Stein, Franziska zu Reventlow, Lou Andreas-Salomé, to name only a few — continues to provoke a desire for understanding. The attempts at such an understanding, however, have so far produced nothing which transcends the private. Katherine Mansfield called this 'the personal', thereby qualifying it.

***

However differing Meyers, Alpers and Tomalin may be — the three, in a stricter sense academic, biographers of the 70s — they reveal the irritation by a subject that, by its own programme, eludes any unifying approach. All three show their fascination with a woman living her sexuality in a way which is accepted as normal with men, but which even today needs to be justified with women.

Meyers[25] knew that Alpers and Tomalin had started their work, and he was determined to publish ahead of them. So he did. Little more needs to be said about this biography today, especially since the (few) reviews have enumerated its obvious mistakes. The kind of subject it creates, the script it writes, still needs to be revealed. In his first biography, where Katherine Mansfield appears as a torn, idiosyncratic, and self-centred character, Alpers had been searching for an interpretive pattern of her personality. He found it in early childhood traumas: the lack of acceptance by her cool mother, the lack of support by her businessman father. This pattern so common in literary criticism of the 50s is still helpful. It is also used by Meyers, who in his book attributes the reason for the tragic course of Katherine Mansfield's life to her want of emotional control and her wish to defy 'social conventions and moral restraints in her quest for love' (p. 32).

For the first time it is not tuberculosis, that fashionable modernist plague, but unrestrained sexual behaviour which is held responsible for the brevity of her life. Schwendimann, Citati, Crone twist Katherine Mansfield's biography until it is socially acceptable; they hide or veil. Meyers errs in the opposite direction. There are many details of the more intimate kind which entirely escaped Meyers and which Alpers was to make public only a short time later. Yet Meyers manages to create Katherine Mansfield in a way that Tomalin was to call 'cynical'. Never resisting temptation when it comes, he pulls in every quote, every bit of text that could prove the extraordinary, or document the 'hard course of loving'. His 'perfect subject' is turned into an object of male curiosity. This is how his — and with it, our — voyeuristic glance never meets the saint, albeit not quite the whore, either. His picture consists of hard lines and sharp angles; there are no redeeming touches, only stark contrasts and strong emotions. The same applies to his presentation of Virginia Woolf, of the relationship between the two women, in fact of any relationship he describes. People are the sum total of facts. Meyers knows, therefore he defines. We get a Katherine Mansfield who is a mixture of Keats and Byron, if without their aim at the absolute: 'The Murrys were middle-class rebels who hated poverty and still believed in marriage, family and home' (p. 72). The hint at such an interesting ambivalence is never followed up, but remains where and as Meyers drops it. Events do not gain in depth as we read; rather, we hurl ourselves against the unexpected and the unusual. This is what makes Meyers' biography romantic in the bad sense of the word. Katherine Mansfield is transfixed as a deviation from the norm, something which she certainly claimed for herself (her belonging to the 'wandering tribe' of the ARTISTS), but which for Meyers is the result only of a lack of emotional control. Even where he does make use of Alpers' pattern of the colonial outsider, he remains within the confines of his own fascination with aberration. This female subject is no more than the inverse of earlier demonstrations of the frail and the pure. Nothing in the large variety of relationships and of figures helps the reader towards forming a clearer pattern of an epoch and its historical dimensions.

This is what Alpers at least tries to establish. Apart from his own classification of biography as either reported, personal, or historical, there is no explicit theoretical framework in Alpers. Still, he is determined to go beyond a mere compilation and combination of text and history. What comes into view are the outlines of an epoch even though they will get blurred by the enormous mass of detail. It is within the horizon of modernity that Alpers firmly roots the unrooted, the outsider — an outsider in quite a different sense than before. Katherine Mansfield now gains her status as one of the essential precursors of modernist literature (all of Woolf's 'great' novels were written after Katherine Mansfield's death). At the same time he demonstrates how her mode of aesthetic perception and articulation depends on a psychic dissociation, to which her sociocultural dissociation gives additional impact.

Alpers, himself a New Zealander and thus a colonial outsider, founds his biography on the double pattern of unfulfilled desire for belonging and of compulsory impersonation. Consequently, the events of spring 1920 with its search for the 'true self' and its 'defeat of the personal' gain enormous weight with Alpers, in contrast to Meyers and even to Tomalin, who both report it as incidental. According to Alpers, Katherine Mansfield was torn between 'two destructive conflicts':

> the love-hate feeling for her father, and the love-hate feeling for her country. They tore her apart in two directions — quartered her, as it were — leaving psychic wounds that would never be healed. (p. 43)

The law-of-the-father (Lacan's terminology springs to mind here even though Alpers does not use it) constitutes the insecurity due to parental rejection, the early experience of the loss of imaginary unity which results in a variety of tentative identities, be it of names or roles; also the use of masks of strength in order to hide insecurity and hurt; these masks deny descent and thereby symbolically kill the father — 'the parricidal use of masks and pseudonyms', (p. 53). This is also where Katherine Mansfield's self-centredness and her lies have their origin, a fact which Dido Davies brings out more clearly than Alpers. In her review of Alpers she says:

> Lies and deceit are symptoms of egocentricity, for they build a new world around the teller who alone knows their truth . . . She soon began to regard her identity as having quite different aspects, separate compartments; the self not divided, but multiplied . . . She was not 'quite determined to be someone else', as Alpers maintains, but was experimenting with the possibilities of her own complex personality. [26]

While Alpers shows a certain tendency towards closure, towards the definitive, Davies insists on the openness of the subject. Nevertheless, Alpers allows the effect of the paternal to include Katherine Mansfield's own ambivalence in sex, her feeling to be, at times, 'more than half man'. And it includes the ambiguity of gender, the ambiguity which women find themselves entangled in once they want to step beyond their conventional sphere. Katherine Mansfield knew very early that she must take and not wait until she was given:

> Here then is a little summary of what I need — power, wealth and freedom. It is the hopelessly insipid doctrine that love is the only thing in the world, taught, hammered into women, from generation to generation, which hampers us so cruelly. We must get rid of that bogey — and then, then comes the opportunity of happiness and freedom.[27]

Alpers quotes this passage which so strongly reminds one of what Virginia Woolf was to write later in her *Room of One's Own*, but, strangely enough, he does not seem to see the parallel. He finds it more important to state that despite such declarations Katherine Mansfield was 'no feminist'. However, the awareness revealing itself in this early diary entry shows her 'feminism' in a much wider sense. Under the same date, May 1908, she also wrote: 'We are firmly held with the self-fashioned chains of slavery. Yes, now I see that they *are* self-fashioned, and must be self-removed.' Trying to remove these chains was to be the battle of her life.

The urge for impersonation, which was painful more often than not, because at its bottom there was always the feeling of hurt and violation and neglect; this and the masks and roles would, in Alpers' view, inevitably lead to Katherine Mansfield's quest for the 'true self, which of my many?' and to the 'defeat of the personal'. Because of his latent desire for the definite, Alpers cannot see that Katherine Mansfield must reject, or try to overcome, 'the personal', for it is constituted by the inauthentic, the ephemeral, and is therefore blind to creative diversity. As he argues himself, it is *vision* rather than *circumstance* that she is after (p. 328). This is also why, in her religious dilemma of 1920, she must reject the personal deity of Christianity. He could only be yet another embodiment of male authenticity and paternal authority.

Katherine Mansfield's psychic disintegration is lent additional force by the rootlessness of the colonial writer. Analysing some early texts, Alpers points out how often women are placed at a window or a door, looking out at the 'other'. 'A trick of the mind is evident: she is constantly inhabiting one space while observing another, and has her characters doing the same' (p. 53). This place at the margin, at the periphery, refers to the second of 'the two destructive conflicts' in Katherine Mansfield's life.[28]

Both insecurities determine Katherine Mansfield's script as Alpers writes it, and they are the token of her place in the aesthetic project of modernity. As a woman, too, one would like to add, although Katherine Mansfield herself would insist that she was 'a writer first and a woman after'; also, it would be unfair towards Alpers to leave it at that. 'But these are all guesses, and only a man's guesses', he says at one point (p. 91). Even though, in the end, he cannot transcend it, he is very much aware of the limitations of his own, male, standpoint, and this awareness is what gives one the impression of reliability in this biography.

Claire Tomalin intended her biography to be guided by such 'woman's guesses'. However, her insights and her new findings remain strangely unconnected with this avowed intention. It is female complicity rather than a feminist perspective that informs her design of a woman's life. Where she does go beyond Alpers is in a historical framing that stresses the female aspect. One of her first chapters is on 'London 1908: New Women'. Her scope broadens when she considers the effects of education and the opportunities women were then gaining: 'A clear pattern emerges of women crossing the barriers of class and defying the sexual conventions' (p. 48). She asks for the determinants of class and sex, not gender. This turns out to be no mere question of terminology. Rather, it points at the main dilemma of her biography, for it restricts her possibility of approaching one of Katherine Mansfield's major concerns, that of identity. Instead, she will remain close to the surface, that of the attractive secret of the love relations. Certainly Tomalin is the first to say something about the role of gonorrhea so fatal for women even of the middle classes in the early decades of this century. The way she does it allows even medically inexperienced readers to understand why Katherine Mansfield could, for such a long time, remain ignorant of the true source of her later illnesses. For Tomalin, by the way, the initial cause is quite clear. Reconsideration of the letters in particular has convinced her of a much closer relationship with Sobieniowski than had been assumed, a closeness which not only brought along the disease, but also the blackmail in 1920. These are doubtless interesting new aspects, and Tomalin presents them in a very convincing way. Still, they only add to what we know; they do not add to a deeper understanding of the personality.

So one looks in vain for some basic pattern or groundwork in Tomalin's approach. Like her predecessors, she mentions Katherine Mansfield's special position within her family and her 'colonial' status, and she talks about lies, deceptions and masks, only to remain with the incidental. The real impulse for Katherine Mansfield's life comes from her 'adventurous spirit' which soon turns into the nemesis of her destiny.

This is the interpretation which Tomalin had already suggested in the introduction to her 1983 edition of the *Short Stories*.[29] The continuing effect of a Victorian pattern of guilt and retribution and the destruction of those women who wanted to be masters of their own fate could perhaps have inspired her to examine the possible impact of such fictional scripts as an ideological pattern that might still be informing lives such as Katherine Mansfield's. This, the division between ideology and individual design, could also help towards an understanding of the contradictions that would arise for women on their way towards emancipation. Clinging to the 'faults' of Katherine Mansfield's early years very nearly aligns Tomalin with Meyers. Of course, not a tinge of his sensationalism colours Tomalin's book; she strives not for contrast, but for mediation and for balance. This, her balanced assessment, is the great achievement of Tomalin's biography. It is most obvious in her presentation of the relationship with Woolf, which — in direct contrast to that by Meyers — sheds a new and elucidating light on these two women and their mutual prejudices as well as their mutual respect.

Tomalin's biography is an extremely readable book. Alpers' book is something of a quarry, while Tomalin's tells a story (it has the additional enticement of an Appendix that gives not only *Leves Amores*, but also the extended public correspondence concerning the question of plagiarism). Alpers and Tomalin unite in one respect: they no longer attempt a one-dimensional picture. Both are led by strong empathy, if not sympathy, with their 'subject' — which need not be a fault even in academic research — but they do not get involved to that point where a clear view is no longer possible; they do not even out the contradictions and fence Katherine Mansfield off as extraordinary; nor do they embellish the ugly and the disgusting. Thus, both have also written honest books.

***

Biography was one form of historiography, from classical times to the 19th century and its positivist re-assessment of history. The genre seems never to have come under theoretical scrutiny, but remained faithful to its own ethos of factual correctness and reliability. Only recently have historians come to recognize the aesthetic quality of their projects. Yet something of the positivist factography, which was contemporaneous with our classic realist texts, still seems to linger in Katherine Mansfield research (even where it is tinged with doubt, as in Alpers or Tomalin), along with the ideological tradition in which we are still steeped:

> The ideology of liberal humanism assumes a world of non-contradictory (and therefore fundamentally unalterable) individuals whose unfettered consciousness is the origin of meaning, knowledge and action. It is in the interest of this ideology . . . to present the individual as a free, unified, autonomous subjectivity.[30]

A different view of women's subjectivity, of the history of women and, by and large, of a new history has been offered by feminist socio-psychologists and historiographers. Re-writing psychoanalysis from Freud through Lacan has led to new theories of female sexuality and subjectivity and revealed the precarious trajectory of women on their way into and through the symbolic order. It has shown that this entry allows self-articulation and also opens up, and puts the lid on, the unconscious. It creates a first division in the subject and thus the need for constant construction and reconstruction of the self, without allowing a coherent social and sexual identity. This analysis of gender and gendered identity has led towards an understanding of the historical construction of (female *and* male) subjectivity that — via deconstruction — transcends the established notions of female subjectivity as the mirror or the reverse of its binary (male) opposite. In an article with the telling title 'Gender: A Useful Category of Historical Analysis', historian Joan Scott says: 'Gender is a way of referring to the exclusively social origins of the subjective identities of men and women. It is a social category imposed on a sexed body.'[31] Adopting Lacaniean theory, with the aim of making its analysis of language a means, not an end, she wants historians to

> examine the ways in which gendered identities are substantively constructed and relate their findings to a range of activities, social organizations, and historically specific cultural representations. The best efforts in this area so far have been, not surprisingly, biographies. (p. 1068)

This, then, could be the new field for Katherine Mansfield biographies — if new ones we need. One step in this direction has already been taken:

> one of the organising principles of the *avant-garde* writing of modernism was centred on a new examination of gender, its origins and its instability. T.S. Eliot's Tiresias, Virginia Woolf's Lily Briscoe and Orlando, Joyce's Leopold Bloom and Katherine Mansfield's Kezia are all examples of this impulse working itself out. Once seen, this important aspect of modernism has clear links with contemporary debates about the nature of gender and with the continuing agitation by women to claim social and political rights. For women writers, there was . . . a 'vital link between experimentation and the need to express a definitive sense of *women's* reality.'[32]

A new tone in Katherine Mansfield criticism. The voice belongs to Kate Fullbrook, who prefaces her textual analyses with some introductory chapters in which she discusses gender and its relation to the major concerns of modernism and explicitly questions notions of the subject and its identity. 'Neat, polarized systems such as Lacan's' she finds insufficient, as well as any other 'retrogressive theories that censor in advance ideas regarding what women might be.' In Fullbrook's understanding, Katherine Mansfield, both in her relationships and in her aesthetics, was trying to escape from the limitations of a socially constructed self, from 'stereotype expectations' (p. 22) that force women into 'a *specific* if not completely knowable self' (p. 25). Katherine Mansfield's impersonations and masks served as a protection for the unstable, fragmented, multiple self. At the other end of her constant covering-up was an 'attraction to a mystic notion of an essential self, discoverable only in moments of spiritual inspiration' (p. 17). While Katherine Mansfield, time and again, would fall into the traps of her gendered identity and while she would articulate her longing for a unified self, she would also, at the same time,

> [resist] her desire to believe in a continuous self that holds the possibilities of release from all roles, masks and fragmentations into a moment of pure being . . . And it is . . . this honest uncertainty in the face of desire and need, that finally makes Katherine Mansfield, at times, one of the toughest and darkest of the modernists. (p. 19)

Fullbrook's few pages of 1986 certainly take us a long way beyond Tomalin's biography of 1987 and point a way out of the factographical dilemma in biography (and, indeed, biographism). Further steps, I think, must be taken if we want to progress beyond the individual and the coincidental. Katherine Mansfield's programmatic multiplication of the self, her refusal of a specific, non-contradictory subjectivity is a sign of her modernism. But was her desire for an essential, 'true', self a sign of an 'attraction to a mystic notion'? Both, I suggest, are signs of a woman's place in (modernist) society, and they were shared by many of her contemporary women artists, whatever their individual fates.[33] So was the lived sexuality of the body and the refusal to see sex in everything. Many shared her life of an exile or, as they seemed to think, the 'return of the native' to their proper home in one of the metropolises of Europe, coming, as they did, from various parts of the 'periphery' and staying and straying with their 'wandering tribe'.

While we have come to read and decipher literary texts and apply to them the latest findings of feminist research, we do yet seem to hesitate to read and decipher the texts of women's lives. And yet, such aesthetic, textualized (not fictionalized!) readings could provide us with biographies that would not be 'definitive' but, rather, opt for a different awareness of the ways and works of the subjects in their participation in, and construction of, the process of history.

NOTES

1. Claire Tomalin, *Katherine Mansfield. A Secret Life* (London: Viking, 1987), p. 5. The book is currently in its third reprint. Tomalin is quoting from Virginia Woolf's diary.

2. Elizabeth Webby, 'Katherine Mansfield: Everything and Nothing', *Meanjin*, 42 (1982), pp. 236-243.

3. Antony Alpers, *The Life of Katherine Mansfield* (London: Jonathan Cape, 1980).

4. C.A. Hankin, *Katherine Mansfield and her Confessional Stories* (London: Macmillan, 1983), p. ix.

5. The following list is by publishers' countries, not by authors' origins. It is certainly not complete. Nelson Wattie is currently preparing an updated bibliography that will provide fuller information.
   In Great Britain and the US: Ruth Elvish Mantz and John Middleton Murry, *The Life of Katherine Mansfield* (London: Constable, 1933); Sylvia Berkman, *Katherine Mansfield: A Critical Study* (London: Oxford University Press, 1952); Antony Alpers, *Katherine Mansfield. A Biography* (New York: A. Knopf, 1953); Jeffrey Meyers, *Katherine Mansfield. A Biography* (London: Hamish Hamilton, 1978); Antony Alpers, *The Life of Katherine Mansfield* (London: Jonathan Cape, 1980); Nora Crone, *A Portrait of Katherine Mansfield* (Ilfracombe, 1985); Claire Tomalin, *Katherine Mansfield. A Secret Life* (London: Viking, 1987).
   In New Zealand, Isabel Clarke, *Katherine Mansfield. A Biography*, ntroduction by P.A. Lawlor (Wellington: The Beltane Book Bureau, 1944), first published as *Six Portraits* (London: 1935); Nelia Gardner White, *Daughter of Time. The Life of Katherine Mansfield in Novel Form* (London: 1942); Robin Hyde (Iris Guiver Wilkinson, 'Katherine Mansfield', see N. Crone, p. 340); Julienne Stretton, *A Portrait of Katherine Mansfield*, 1986; John Reid, *Leave All Fair*, 1986.
   In France, Odette Lenoël, *La vocation de Katherine Mansfield* (Paris: Albin Michel, 1946); Roland Merlin, *Le drame secret de Katherine Mansfield* (Paris: Seuil, 1950); A.-M. Monnet, *Katherine Mansfield* (Paris: Les Editions du Temps, 1960); Michel Dupuis, *Katherine Mansfield* (Paris: La Manufacture, 1988); P.-A. Hauvette, 'Ode à Katherine Mansfield', *L'Auvergne Littéraire* (Clermont-Ferrant, 1967); Monique Fabre, *Le deuil éclatant du bonheur. Prélude à Katherine Mansfield* (Paris, 1983); Alexis Salatko, *S'il pleut, il pleuvra* (Paris: Presses de la Renaissance, 1987). For the French reception see the article by Christiane Mortelier, 'Origine et développement d'une légende. Katherine Mansfield en France', *Etudes Anglaises*, 23 (1970), pp. 357-368.
   In West Germany, Max Schwendimann, *Katherine Mansfield, ihr*

Leben in Darstellung und Dokumentation (München, 1967); Christa Moog, *Aus tausend grünen Spiegeln* (Düsseldorf, 1988).
In Austria, Erwin Einzinger, *Kopfschmuck für Katherine Mansfield* (Salzburg/Wien, 1985).
In Italy, Pietro Citati, *Vita breve di Katherine Mansfield* (Milano: Rizzoli, 1980). Translated into German by Dora Winkler, *Katherine Mansfield. Beschreibung eines Lebens* (Frankfurt, 1982); translated into French by Brigitte Pérol, *Brève vie de Katherine Mansfield* (Paris: Quai Voltaire, 1987).

6. Antony Alpers, ed., *The Stories of Katherine Mansfield. Definitive Edition* (Oxford: Oxford University Press, 1984).

7. Antony Alpers, 'Biography — the "Scarlet Experiment"', *TLS* (28.3.1980), p. 370b.

8. Dennis Mceldowney, 'The Multiplex Effect: Recent Biographical Writing on Katherine Mansfield', *Ariel*, 16, 4 (1985), p. 111.

9. Marvin Magalaner, 'Traces of her "Self" in Katherine Mansfield's "Bliss"', *Modern Fiction Studies*, 24 (1978), p. 413.

10. Sidney Cox, 'The Fastidiousness of Katherine Mansfield', *Sewanee Review*, 39 (1931), pp. 158-169.

11. Clare Hanson, ed., *The Critical Writings of Katherine Mansfield* (London: Macmillan, 1987), p. 2.

12. A letter dated 24 April 1906!, in *The Collected Letters of Katherine Mansfield*, edited by Vincent O'Sullivan and Margaret Scott, vol. 1 (Oxford: Oxford University Press, 1984), p. 19.

13. *Katherine Mansfield. Letters and Journals. A Selection*, edited by C.K. Stead (Harmondsworth: Penguin, 1978), p. 173.

14. Edward Wagenknecht, 'Katherine Mansfield', *English Journal*, 17 (1928), p. 272.

15. Alpers, *Life*, p. 308.

16. Tomalin, p. 227. C.K. Stead voices a similar opinion, cp. his *In a Glass Case. Essays on New Zealand Literature* (Auckland/Oxford, University Press, 1981), p. 22.

17. Arnold Whitridge, 'Katherine Mansfield', *Sewanee Review*, 48 (1940), p. 256.

18. See Tomalin: 'Her short life, so modern and busy, has the shape of a classic tragedy . . . If she was never a saint, she was certainly a martyr, and a heroine in her recklessness, her dedication and her courage' (p. 243).

19. Cp. Mortelier, p. 364 and M.L. Cazamian's review of Alpers in *Etudes Anglaises*, 8 (1955), p. 167: 'Il reste une limite à observer,

pour s'en tenir aux faits significatifs, c'est-à-dire ceux qui se reflètent directement dans l'oeuvre. Le détail de ses aventures sexuelles, de sa vie amoureuse complexe, ardente ou refoulée; le cours troublé de l'amitié féminine inlassablement dévouée dont elle a usé et abusé — tout cela aurait pu être tu, puisque son effort a consisté à s'en émanciper, et à garder ses écrits purs, brillants et radieux.'

Cp. also Arthur Mizener in *Kenyon Book Review*, 16 (1953), p. 136: 'Though understanding is always a satisfaction, it can also be, as in this case, something of a shock.' A new approach in French Mansfield biographies has now been taken by Michel Dupuis in his 1988 biography.

20. Berkman's book appeared in 1951 and combines biography and textual analysis.

21. 'Il est permis de penser que de telles affirmations, jaillies des profondeurs d'une des âmes les plus douloureuses et les plus pures qui aient fleuri ici-bas doivent trouver un écho indéfini chez tous ceux qui s'efforcent en tâtonnant de retrouver le chemin perdu de l'unité intérieure', he wrote in a review 'Katherine Mansfield', *Revue Hebdomadaire* (11.7.1931), p. 181.

22. Schwendimann, p. 249.

23. Whereas the German translation at least gives a general reference to the *Journal* and the stories, the Italian only uses frequent quotation marks without ever giving a hint as to where these borrowings come from.

24. The crystal also appears in Citati and seems to serve for various purposes: the crystal pane of distance, the crystallization of love (hearking back to Stendhal?), the crystal pane that constitutes her grandeur, etc.

25. Jeffrey Meyers, 'The Quest for Katherine Mansfield', *Biography. An Interdisciplinary Quarterly*, 1 (1978), p. 52.

26. Dido Davies, 'Self-Absorbed. *The Life of Katherine Mansfield* by Antony Alpers', *Essays in Criticism*, 32 (1982), p. 195.

27. *Journal of Katherine Mansfield*, edited by John Middleton Murry (London: Constable, 1954), p. 37.

28. See Alpers, p. 43. It might prove fruitful to think this over in terms of Wallerstein's concepts of 'center' and 'periphery'.

29. Katherine Mansfield, *Short Stories*, edited by Claire Tomalin (London: Dent, 1983).

30. Catherine Belsey, 'Constructing the subject: deconstructing the text', in *Feminist Criticism and Social Change*, edited by Deborah Rosenfelt and Judith Newton (London: Methuen, 1985), p. 51.

31. Joan W. Scott, 'Gender: A Useful Category of Historical Analysis', *American Historical Review*, 91 (1986), pp. 1053-1075.

32. Kate Fullbrook, *Katherine Mansfield* (Brighton: The Harvester Press, 1986), p. 12. In his 1985 dissertation *Vorbereitung der Moderne. Aspekte erzählerischer Gestaltung in den Kurzgeschichten von James Joyce und Katherine Mansfield* (Bern: Lang, 1986), Jochen Ganzmann regrets feminist appropriations of Katherine Mansfield. He bases his objections on recent editions of Katherine Mansfield's texts by women, but does not give one single example of a feminist interpretation. Fullbrook's book was not yet out. Thus, feminism as a scandalon seems to blossom where it has not even taken root.

33. See Belsey, p. 50.

LIVING AND WRITING

Katherine Mansfield:
Subjection and Authority

KATE FULLBROOK

In her fiction, Katherine Mansfield was openly, even obsessively, concerned with the condition of women. Story after story takes as its subject paradigmatic moments in the lives of usually suffering women. Devastatingly honest about the games women play and the lies they tell themselves to hold themselves in their various marginalized cultural places, Katherine Mansfield shows women as repressed, victimized, excluded, and often caught in roles they neither want nor understand. Katherine Mansfield nevertheless writes of women with compassion as well as clarity of vision and implicitly condemns the dominant structures — economic, educational, relational, psychological — which keep her women baffled, exploited, and in pain.

This tendency in the fiction, its passionate presentation of women's lives carrying an explicit moral condemnation of their position, is blindingly obvious. Yet as a writer, Katherine Mansfield thought of herself as genderless. She called herself simply and repeatedly an 'artist', complained of publicity that stressed her skill as a 'woman writer', and was adamantly scornful of the idea of a separate, modernist, female prose.[1]

Katherine Mansfield's refusal to welcome the label of woman writer is related closely to her ideas about the construction of gender. For her, masculine and feminine are not fixed, singular, or normative terms, and not in the possession of members of either biological sex. Even the most positive metaphorical ascription of the term 'feminine' to the kind of prose modernists were evolving — fluid, oblique, and full of logical surprises — was for her a misleading gesture. One simply cannot imagine Katherine Mansfield isolating and glorifying a notion like Virginia Woolf's 'woman's sentence'.[2] And as Clare Hanson has pointed out, she specifically and publicly attacked contemporary proponents of 'feminine prose' in her reviews of novels by Dorothy Richardson and May Sinclair.[3]

This disjunction between a fiction that is radically committed to an oppositional view of women and an aesthetic that rejects definition in terms of gender is a recurrent phenomenon among twentieth-century women writers; a strategy used at times by writers as disparate as Virginia Woolf herself, with her influential call for androgyny, to Doris Lessing, whose notorious refusal of identification of feminist intentions in the introduction to *The Golden Notebook* is placed side by side with an avowal of commitment to many of the ideals of the movement itself.[4]

What I want to do in this paper is to look at this apparent contradiction in Katherine Mansfield's thought and work, and to argue that such a position in fact represents a strong claim for women writers as architects of consciousness, contributors to ideological change through the revision of dominant ways of understanding.

That Katherine Mansfield understood, from an early age, the major outlines of the subjection of women is not in dispute. Parts of her reaction to Elizabeth Robins' *Come and Find Me* in 1908 are worth noting again:

> I have just finished reading a book by Elizabeth Robins, *Come and Find Me*. Really, a clever, splendid book; it creates in me such a sense of power. I feel that I do now realize, dimly, what women in the future will be capable of. They truly as yet have never had their chance. Talk of our enlightened days and our emancipated country — pure nonsense! We are firmly held with the self-fashioned chains of slavery. Yes, now I see that they are self-fashioned, and must be self-removed.[5]

The programme that the nineteen-year-old Katherine Mansfield sets for herself — 'independence, resolve, firm purpose, and the gift of discrimination, *mental clearness* . . . Will . . . power, wealth and freedom' — matches with exactness the life of the New Woman that she was so shortly to embark upon, and which, without control of her reproductive capabilities or of the venereal disease that was to torment and undermine her, was to end in such personal disaster.[6] And yet, she was entirely serious about the need for change for women and that seriousness shows itself throughout her fiction as well as in her life. The catalogue of needs of 1908 constitutes a list of the things that damage her women characters because of their absence. And perhaps the most significant thing to note in Katherine Mansfield's early account of the position of women is its insistence on the importance of the future. She is noting need, and her emphasis is on bringing into being something which is as yet dimly understood. And, as Simone de Beauvoir was later to emphasize, the responsibility for bringing about this change rested with women themselves.

At the same time it must be noted that Katherine Mansfield was, to say the least, less than wholly enthusiastic about the strategies of contemporary feminism. She was equally willing to satirize the suffrage movement in England, with its trust in legal reform of women's lot, and its suspicion of anything that might be labelled as traditionally feminine, as she was to mock early twentieth-century versions of female triumphalism. What she was looking for were not variants of pre-existing social paradigms but a revolution in social consciousness, and how she, as a writer, might help to effect such a revolution. To see what she had in mind it is necessary to look at her most significant account of the relationship between the artist and society.

The following passage appears in her *Journal* for November 1921 and comes as part of a response to Vaihinger's *Die Philosophie des Als Ob*. It is Katherine Mansfield's clearest mature statement of what she conceived of as the nature of the intersection of the material world and the activity of the writer in relation to that world.

> Why must thinking and existing be ever on two different planes? Why will the attempt of Hegel to transform subjective processes into objective world-processes not work out? 'It is the special art and object of thinking to attain existence by quite other methods than that of existence itself.' That is to say, reality cannot become the ideal, the dream; and it is not the business of the artist to grind an axe, to try to impose his vision of life upon the existing world. Art is not an attempt of the artist to reconcile existence with his vision; it is an attempt to create his own world in this world. That which suggests the subject to the artist is the *unlikeness* to what we accept as reality. We single out — we bring into the light — we put up higher.[7]

This is a difficult and not entirely coherent statement, and it is obvious that Katherine Mansfield is struggling to clarify for herself a central question about the purpose of art. There are, however, aspects of the journal entry which need to be noted, and which have a direct bearing on what she was trying to do in her fictional treatment of women. First, there is her insistence on the existence of writing as a part of the world itself. It is not a thing apart, not a fragment of some romantic, ideal, absolute other place, but part of 'this world'. And this materially existent writing calls into being what Henry James called 'the possible other case'. It addresses what the writer and the reader are prepared to accept and acknowledge as the nature of the world. From this point of view the writer's work involves the change of 'acceptance' of the fixity of circumstances by implying or showing alternative possibilities. It is an account of a method that works on the consciousness of the reader by undermining prior certainties about the nature of the world. The method outlined is indirectly didactic, immensely supple, and altogether absorbed in effective disruption of the way things are perceived to be.

Katherine Mansfield's refusal of the title of woman writer can be seen as one such disruption. The negative side of such a disclaimer may be a rejection of solidarity with other women, a probably deluded claim for separate, privileged treatment. The positive side of the refusal marks a claim for the general importance of writing by women for women and men alike in mapping the terrain of what are and are not conscious versions of the world that deserve acceptance. It puts women's writing on an equal footing with men's writing, and claims for her own writing, so closely attuned to the experience of women and to ways of representing and interpreting that experience that are other than the traditional ones, the kind of full validity and power that men writers always have, and still do, take for granted. I think that it is possible to argue that this is one of the most radically feminist claims that it is possible for a writer to make.

The way in which these revisionary impulses to change the status of the woman writer coalesced with a passionate investigation into women's experience in Katherine Mansfield's work can only be understood through looking at the fiction itself. In the second part of this paper, I want to look at Katherine Mansfield's technique in an early and a late story in the light of the attempt to create an alternative world in this world. The stories with which I will be concerned are 'The Swing of the Pendulum' from the 1911 *German Pension* collection and 'A Cup of Tea' which first appeared in *Storyteller* in 1922, and which was collected in *The Dove's Nest* in 1923. Both stories are attuned to women's consciousness at moments of confusion, desperation, and ambivalence. Both show female characters imagining themselves into alternative identities, and, at the last moment, pulling back from change and self-knowledge. These tales of how change fails to happen are intimately concerned with material pressures, and both stress particular cultural factors that hold women in place and inhibit them from facing the unhappy nature of their circumstances. The two stories concern themselves with the operation of traditional ideologies about women in the consciousnesses of women themselves. Both are revelatory, instructive, and work to disrupt the reader's expectations of the ways in which women think and feel, and of the kinds of confused and contradictory pressures under which they typically live. The circumstances of the stories, in their different ways, circle around those two most important issues for women — love and money — and in each case Katherine Mansfield writes in an ironic prose that is a reflection of, and a commentary on, the kinds of false consciousness she diagnoses as classically working in her characters.

The strategies of the modernist prose of the first part of the twentieth century have still not lost their power to surprise, to disrupt and subvert readers' expectations, their patterns of 'acceptance'. The full force of this power has, of course, been lost along with the historical moment of its development. But it is worth stressing again the place of indirectness in this writing, the crucial importance of the symbol, of the words not quite said, of the idea implied to the reader but left unrevealed and stated within the text itself. For many key modernist women — and here one must include Katherine Mansfield with Richardson, Woolf, and Stein[8] — this indirectness in writing was repeatedly allied with their identification of the unknown, the unsaid, the hidden as a constituent part of the condition of women. The aesthetic pressure comes, at least in part, from the struggle to find a literary equivalent for this specific aspect of experience.

In this light 'The Swing of the Pendulum' is one of the most telling of the early stories in terms of watching Katherine Mansfield feel her way toward the development of her thematic and technical strengths. Whereas most of the *Pension* stories are frankly sarcastic in tone, and place the centre of consciousness and analytical poise in a privileged first-person narrator who is transparently close to being a partial autobiographical variant of the author, 'The Swing of the Pendulum' uses quite different tactics. The narrative position is unstable — Katherine Mansfield inflects her basic third-person narration with symbolist gestures, incisive reportage of flickers of consciousness, and intermittant use of the indirect free style. All are attuned to the portrayal of the confusion of Viola, the central character, who is caught in a dangerous situation of impending personal disaster, and who strains to think her way out of her trouble by manipulating various clichés of women's sexual power. Alone in her room, which she scarcely dares to leave, Viola is one of those imprisoned women characters who constitutes such a recognizable thematic obsession in Katherine Mansfield's stories and in women's fiction in general. The story takes place on the razor's edge of psychological disintegration. Viola is destitute; this is the source of her distress, and the puzzles she needs to solve to free herself are all related to money. Viola is also a writer, one who has difficulties in getting anything published, and who has no faith in her own work as a means to financial salvation. Instead her material need translates into an internal debate about two possible relational positions to men, both grounded in the need to annex a man as a source of wealth. Viola hides this fundamental impulse from herself in thick overlays of glamour as she reflects on the kind of commodity she should choose to be in the heterosexual market-place.

The character aches for material luxury, but she also longs for heroism. The two opposing roles she consciously fingers both situate her in relation to these two needs. The first role is the one she is already unhappily enacting — that of the sacrificial ideal lover of her exotically named artist, Casimir. Unfortunately, Casimir is as unsuccessful as a writer as Viola, and sacrifice, for her, is not as thrilling as she thought it might be. While hard living for the sake of art inspires her with a voyeuristic pleasure at her own secular martyrdom, Viola has also imagined such sacrifice as purely temporary. As she waits for the pointedly non-appearing Casimir, she has a fit of honesty after she has considered an implausible method of suicide as a way out of her dilemma:

> I was not in love. I wanted somebody to look after me — and keep me until my work began to sell — and he kept bothers with other men away. . . . And I believed in him then. I thought his work had only to be recognised once, and he'd roll in wealth. I thought perhaps we might be poor for a month — but he said, if only he could have me, the stimulus. . . . Funny, if it wasn't so damned tragic! (p. 83)

Viola's alternate solution is figured by the appearance of a 'strange man' at her door. The second role she imagines is also a survival strategy, also smothered in glamour. Viola recognizes that Casimir cannot save her and her desperation deepens:

> 'what should I do then — where should I go to?' There was nowhere. 'I don't want to work — or carve out my own path. I want ease and any amount of nursing in the lap of luxury. There is only one thing I'm fitted for, and that is to be a great courtesan.' (p. 84)

Imagining herself into this role, Viola tries to seduce the strange man while at the same time turning the prospect of common prostitution — a quick trick in a cheap lodging house — into a fantasy of herself as a *grande horizontale*. It doesn't work; she panics at her own audacity. Another irrelevant self-definition, that of the outraged 'respectable' woman, takes hold as Viola throws the man out and returns to her alternate fantasy as the heroic beloved of the still absent Casimir. She is keeping faith with shadows, with unstable self-representations of womanly virtue, held in her room by a threatening landlady in a text that bristles with the language of money which, like Casimir, remains overpoweringly unavailable.

The triad of sexuality, money, and fantasy dominates this tale of a young woman's desperation as she plays with the counters of women's classic roles, none of which apply to her own situation. Katherine Mansfield gets her effects with a conjunction of realist techniques with those of allegory — the strange man remains unnamed, as does the landlady who, dragon-like, signals the division between women, as well as the dominance of even the most petty manifestation of secure material power over the helplessness of the woman without money. The tale focuses on the way that material need deforms and even blocks women's channels of sexual desire. The dirty and slender pack of women's dreams that Viola rifles through looking for the winning card for her circumstances only contains losers. But the story suggests alternative strategies of responsibility for oneself, financial control as a precondition for love, the need to renounce glamour for realistic appraisal of circumstances as necessary for the solution of Viola's womanly dilemma at the same time as it enacts the strengths of psychological patterns of aspiration and self-definition that the female character does not completely question even *in extremis*.

'A Cup of Tea' moves along the same continuum of conjoined ideas, placing a woman's financial dependence at the centre of her problematic sense of identity and confusions of desire. In this story, published over a decade after 'The Swing of the Pendulum', Katherine Mansfield is in full control of her symbolist resources, and the brilliant strokes of compound meaning and suggestion work subliminally to reproduce in the reader's consciousness the inarticulate confusions that the story implies. The title of the story is a case in point. Its quiet ordinariness carries covert associations both with a lady's leisured delicacies and with the traditional English street beggar's pleas for the most basic sustenance and comfort. These associations of material polarization are evoked in various ways in the story, and the tilting ambivalence of the title bears directly on the substance of the text.

The central character's flowery post-lapsarian name, Rosemary Fell, has, like Viola's name in 'The Swing of the Pendulum', Shakespearian resonances. Shipwrecked Viola in *Twelfth Night* carries associations of disaster and sexual disguise; rosemary belongs to the mad Ophelia, who distributes it to the royal party as a token of remembrance. In her way, Rosemary Fell is a twentieth-century aristocrat. Abundance, modernity, success, and assured assertiveness as the surrogate consumer of her husband's significant wealth are her first defining attributes in the tale. The breathless, fashionable narrative voice, in exact duplication of Rosemary's consciousness, slips into tentativeness only when her uncertain beauty is described. Rosemary worries a lot about her looks. The story begins and ends with her questioning of their effectiveness and the course of the story slowly unveils the significance of this interrogation.

Rosemary has reached the state where she exists only through her purchases. At her 'special' antique shop, with its flattering shopkeeper, she sees something she wants but which, because of the price, even Rosemary hesitates to buy. The object, a tiny, fragile box with an impossibly fine enamel glaze has a picture of a minute woman on its diminutive lid. It is frightfully expensive and is, of course, in all its significant detail, an emblem of Rosemary's own expensive and frighteningly vulnerable life. Rosemary leaves the box in the shop, though she longs to possess it, to 'cling to' it, and enters the real world of cold, winter rain. In this unprotected and savage world she is approached by a young woman who begs her for 'the price of a cup of tea'.[9] And as Rosemary turns in relief from her own wistful dissatisfaction she builds on the theoretical possibilities of the situation for adventure, altruism, and the chance to see herself in a new way:

> And suddenly it seemed to Rosemary such an adventure. It was like something out of a novel by Dostoevsky, this meeting in the dusk. Supposing she took the girl home? Supposing she did do one of those things she was always reading about in stories or seeing on the stage, what would happen? It would be thrilling. (p. 411)

The girl, 'Miss Smith' (a penniless everywoman figure clearly related to Rosemary's own unease), is taken home as Rosemary reads a programme of radical social transformation into her thrilling gesture.

> She was going to prove to this girl that — wonderful things did happen in life, that — fairy godmothers were real, that — rich people had hearts, and that women *were* sisters. She turned impulsively, saying: 'Don't be frightened. After all, why shouldn't you come back with me? We're both women. If I'm the more fortunate, you ought to expect . . .' (p. 411)

Her analysis is more correct than Rosemary cares to acknowledge to herself, and her utopian plan is speedily abandoned when her husband notes the beauty of the girl after she has been relieved of her near starvation. In response, Rosemary throws her out and begs money from her husband for the extravagant little box after all. The story ends with Rosemary begging for his assurance that she is 'still pretty'.

This plea for a reassuring appraisal of her sexual market value combined with Rosemary's cruelty to the girl as she ends her tiny experiment in social justice and calls pathetically for firm possession of the tiny enamel box of her exquisite existence makes the story a bitter and clear-sighted statement about the antagonism of women as rivals for the attachment of men with money. Rosemary, of course, understands nothing of her motivations and remembers nothing of the alternative possibilities with which she flirted for an instant. The reader, however, is drawn into critical analysis of the cynical action.

What I hope has become obvious in these accounts of 'The Swing of the Pendulum' and 'A Cup of Tea' is the way in which Katherine Mansfield's literary strategies are attuned to revealing the intersection of economic helplessness and the various kinds of psychological distress experienced by women. Both of these stories appear, at first glance, to show women as flighty, insubstantial, untrustworthy. They seem to be representations of women's unreliability. But the burden of the stories, in their controlled composition, and in their significant suggestions, shows women as responding reasonably to intolerable pressures. The situations, not the women, are impossible. This is not ambivalence but critical reappraisal of some commonplace interpretations of the behaviour and attitudes of women. The hard-headed analysis of the confusions, and the complexities of the female characters' reactions to them are informed by Katherine Mansfield's characteristically pressing need to suggest that things might be otherwise. In addressing herself continually to these kinds of issues, and signalling their oblique but ubiquitous importance through a prose that is itself oblique and multiply suggestive, and by making available for examination the kinds of distortions and evasions that enmesh her characters, Katherine Mansfield does indeed work to demonstrate the 'unlikeness' of what could be accepted as a decent position for women when compared to what we still accept as reality.

NOTES

1. See, for example, *Katherine Mansfield's Letters to John Middleton Murry: 1913-1922,* edited by John Middleton Murry (London: Constable, 1951), p. 614.

2. *A Room of One's Own,* 1929, reprinted (Harmondsworth: Penguin, 1977), pp. 72-4.

3. See Clare Hanson, 'Introduction', *The Critical Writings of Katherine Mansfield* (London: Macmillan, 1987), pp. 17-20.

4. *A Room of One's Own,* pp. 93-4; Doris Lessing, *The Golden Notebook,* (New York: Bantam, 1973), pp. viii-ix.

5. *Journal of Katherine Mansfield,* edited by John Middleton Murry (London: Constable, 1954), p. 36.

6. *Journal,* p. 37.

7. Ibid., p. 273.

8. Sydney Janet Kaplan, 'Katherine Mansfield's "Passion for Technique" ' in *Women's Language and Style,* edited by D. Butturff and E.L. Epstein, *Studies in Contemporary Language,* n° 1 (Akron, Ohio: University of Akron, 1978), pp. 119-131.

9. *Collected Stories of Katherine Mansfield,* (London: Constable, 1945), p. 410. The other page references to this story are to this edition and are given in the text. The story is omitted in A. Alpers' edition (see his 'commentary' p. 576).

Katherine Mansfield's Life as a Work of Art

CLARE HANSON

When Katherine Mansfield's second book, *Bliss and Other Stories*, was published in 1920, she was both amused and angry about the promotion which her book received — the blurb, the dust-jacket and so on. She wrote:

> Just while I'm on the subject I suppose you will think I am an egocentric to mind the way Constable has advertised my book and the paragraph that is on the paper cover. I'd like to say that I mind so terribly that there are no words for me. No — I'm DUMB!! I think it so insulting and disgusting and undignified that — well — there you are! It's no good suffering all over again. But the bit about 'Women will learn by heart and not repeat'. Gods! why didn't they have a photograph of me looking through a garter. But I was helpless here — too late to stop it — so now I *must* prove — no, convince people ce n'est pas moi.[1]

Katherine Mansfield objected particularly to the way in which she was being presented as a woman and as a writer, about the way in which her sex was being used to sell the book to a secret society, as it were, of women readers who would, significantly, 'not repeat' whatever they learnt from it. Katherine Mansfield expresses her anger at the way in which she and her readers are not only confined to a female ghetto but also patronized and robbed of effective speech — for effective speech is surely that which promotes response, dialogue or action, not silence.

The doubtless unwitting reduction of value and reputation carried out by Constable in 1920 has been repeated many times in the history of Katherine Mansfield criticism. She has consistently been viewed and presented as a woman's writer, possessing what are thought to be the peculiarly feminine attributes of delicacy, sensitivity and so on,[2] and it has been implied that her scope and 'seriousness' as a writer are in some way compromised because her fiction is largely confined to the domestic sphere.[3] In this respect, we may compare critical judgements of Elizabeth Bowen and Rosamund Lehmann, from, broadly, Katherine Mansfield's own period and, more recently, of Elizabeth Taylor or Barbara Pym.

There should be no need for me to rehearse here the feminist arguments against the idea that particular qualities may be viewed as essentially or naturally feminine, nor for me to make again the point that the deeper things of life are as much present in the private as in the public sphere, in the drawing room as on the battlefield. As Virginia Woolf put it in *A Room of One's Own,*

> it is obvious that the values of women differ very often from the values which have been made by the other sex; naturally [?], this is so. Yet it is the masculine values that prevail. Speaking crudely, football and sport are 'important'; the worship of fashion, the buying of clothes 'trivial'. And these values are inevitably transferred from life to fiction. This is an important book, the critic assumes, because it deals with war. This is an insignificant book because it deals with the feelings of women in a drawing-room. A scene in a battle — field is more important than a scene in a shop — everywhere and much more subtly the difference of value persists.[4]

As you may guess, I find it extremely tempting to press these issues in relation to the status of Katherine Mansfield's fiction, which I believe to be undervalued for a complex of gender-related reasons. However, I want in this paper to focus on another aspect of Katherine Mansfield's work, one in which many of the same issues are, however, at stake. I want to consider aspects of Katherine Mansfield's creation of her life as a work of art for public consumption. This is, I confess at the outset, a slippery and difficult subject, fraught with methodological problems. How can we separate the 'life' which we know from the letters and notebooks from the 'portrait of a lady' built up by Murry in his introductions to editions of the *Letters, Journal(s)* and *Scrapbook?* How can we separate both of these 'lives' of Katherine Mansfield from the detailed biographical accounts which began to appear as early as 1933? What distinction do we make between these biographical accounts and her life and personality as presented in the fiction and memoirs of contemporaries? The problems are immense, but I think it is worth making one fundamental point before going on to these delicate areas. I would suggest that the presentation of Katherine Mansfield's life as a work of art fits in with a pattern particularly prevalent in the Modernist period, though it is not of course confined to it. Sandra M. Gilbert and Susan Gubar have suggested in *No Man's Land,* the first volume of their feminist-literary-historical review of the period, that male Modernist writers fetishized the production of abstruse and 'impersonal' texts to the point where attitudes and values conventionally held to be 'feminine' were virtually excluded from their work.[5] In such a situation, I suggest, the life of the woman writer took on a new significance. Turned away from the palace of art, the woman writer took refuge in her 'life' as an area of expression or image-creation left wholly open to her. It was in a sense a new area of expression because of the loosening of certain sexual taboos. It is striking, then, to see how many women writers of this period invested much energy in the creation of emblematic (usually 'bohemian') lives: Jean Rhys, H.D. and Djuna Barnes are parallel figures who come to mind. It is often suggested that the art of these women suffered, and perhaps this may be so — but I think it is also possible that we need to look at the relation between life and art in a new light. Perhaps we need to recognize that the 'life' in these cases is as much a valid cultural construct as the 'art' — and one open to similar techniques of analysis.

Autobiographical writing was of course one major means by which Katherine Mansfield created a life of Katherine Mansfield. Throughout her life she created a self at one remove, as it were, through her notebooks and letters, intending this self-portrait to be offered to the public for consumption. This was an intention, however, which could remain hidden even from herself, as perhaps it had to be, for whatever one's need for self-expression, it has never been easy for women to claim the right to such expression in cold print. Autobiographical writing attracted Katherine Mansfield, I suggest, for the same reasons as it has attracted other women: precisely because of its ambiguous status, because of its existence on the borderline between public and private worlds. It was the sort of writing which Katherine Mansfield could, consciously at least, consider 'private' — though on more than one occasion she did consider writing a 'journal' for publication. On a deeper, less conscious level, this work was intended for an audience, but it was an audience which could remain virtual, undefined, ideal. This accounts for a particular quality of this writing, the strong feeling it gives of being produced for its own sake, without the constraints of audience/genre expectations. This quality is intensified in the later autobiographical work, in which I include her letters to Murry, because of her awareness of the nearness of death: the knowledge that she was writing almost literally in the dark, for an audience she would never see, shadows these texts. The complex interrelations between writing and mortality, or between writing and/as life, are made almost palpable in this journal entry of 1920:

> Oh, to be a *writer*, a real writer given up to it and to it alone! Oh, I failed to day; I turned back, looked over my shoulder, and immediately it happened, I felt as though I too were struck down. The day turned cold and dark on the instant. It seemed to belong to summer twilight in London, to the clang of the gates as they close the garden, to the deep light painting the high houses, to the smell of leaves and dust, to the lamp-light, to that stirring of the senses, to the langour of twilight, the breath of it on one's cheek, to all those things which (I feel to-day) are gone from me for ever .... [6]

Before going on to other facets of Katherine Mansfield's life as a work of art, I would like to make two points about this autobiographical writing. The first is really an argument for its importance as the testimony of a woman writer in the early years of the century. Many women writers have shrunk from placing an artist at the centre of their work (Virginia Woolf, Dorothy Richardson, for example), but in her letters and journals, half-fictionalized as they are, Katherine Mansfield gives us a detailed picture of the developing consciousness of an early twentieth-century woman writer: the portrait may be compared with that of Anna Wulf in Doris Lessing's similarly fragmented later twentieth-century text, *The Golden Notebook*.

The second point has to be more tentative because it involves questions of value. I would like to suggest that Katherine Mansfield's letters and journals should be viewed not, as they commonly are, as ancillary material, but as literary texts to be valued in their own right. Autobiographical writing of this nature is clearly far more than documentary. I have tried to suggest something of the complexity of its position, existing as it does in a no-man's land between fact and fiction, public and private worlds. Katherine Mansfield's autobiographical writing deserves more recognition and more attention, particularly at a time when such writing by other women is being re-viewed and, as it were, upgraded. The Diary and the life/death of Alice James is an example. Letter, diary and journal material is of course almost paradigmatically 'feminine' in its formal disjointedness, its apparently ephemeral quality, its concern with the everyday: hence, perhaps, the lowly status of autobiographical writing in the hierarchy of genres.

Katherine Mansfield began the construction of her autobiographical self-portrait at an early age, certainly before 1903; the process went on, in different ways, until her death. This 'life' which we have come to know from the letters and journals may be distinguished in many ways from the 'real-life' drama of her existence. I have suggested that Katherine Mansfield was like many women artists of her time in attempting to turn her 'lived existence' into a work of art: several reasons may be adduced for this attempt. Katherine Mansfield initially took the belief that one's life should be shaped as a work of art from Pater and Wilde, writers who both had something to hide in terms of gender orientation. One might suggest that it was anxiety about gender-identity which led Pater and Wilde to adopt particular roles and masks; further, that the anxiety which they felt about the relation between their suspect masculine identity and their art prefigured many of the anxieties Katherine Mansfield felt. Early twentieth-century women writers such as Katherine Mansfield were attempting to establish themselves as professional artists in a new sense: they wanted to be accepted as fellow *workers* on a par with male counterparts. Yet they were perceived and perceived themselves as inadequate on the grounds of one of the most fundamental constituents of their identity: their gender. It was gender which made it difficult — as it had been difficult for Pater and Wilde — to take and claim the authority/authoritativeness associated with 'the artist'. It was also difficult for women to affirm that their ('trivial', warned Woolf) perspectives were as valid as those of male artists, with their claim to a monopoly on the 'universal' perspective.

Gillian Hanscombe and Virginia L. Smyers, in *Writing for Their Lives*, discuss some of the difficulties facing women artists in the early years of the century. They note the prevailing sense that there was something anomalous in being both a woman and an artist, and ascribe this feeling to a cultural conflict between the role of 'good woman' (unselfish lover/wife/mother) and 'good artist' (a writer 'never takes second place voluntarily', they write).[7] They suggest that it was in order to resolve the conflict between being a 'real woman' and a 'real writer' that many women writers of the period took their art into their lives, 'wishing [their] creative energy to take every form of expression possible to [them]'. This is clearly partly true in Katherine Mansfield's case. The events leading up to her miscarriage in Germany in 1909, for example, offer a painful instance of a woman leading an irregular, bohemian life in order to try to bring to-

Katherine Mansfield c. 1921

gether parts of her being which seemed irreconcilable: her sense of herself as an artist and her sense of herself as a biological woman. Yet the position is still more complicated in her case because the bohemian life style was in itself a kind of mask: Katherine Mansfield did not often take her art into her life as fully as the mask might suggest. She retained a core, as it were, of conventionality. After 1918, the possibilities of her life were severely circumscribed by the constraints of her illness. There was little room for outrageous behaviour although she could wear outrageous perfume;[8] the art of life began to fine itself down to the kind of care for design noted by Woolf in a description of a visit to Portland Villas in Hampstead:

> Everything was very tidy, bright, & somehow like a doll's house. At once, or almost, we got out of shyness. She (it was summer) half lay on the sofa by the window. She had her look of a Japanese doll, with the fringe combed quite straight across her forehead. . . . She looked very ill — very drawn, & moved languidly, drawing herself across the room, like some suffering animal.[9]

Katherine Mansfield's pursuit of drama and style in her 'real life' thus accords in the earlier part of her career with the account given by Hanscombe and Smyers of the transgressive behaviour of women artists attempting to heal the split between their lives and avant-garde art. Later, I suggest, her cultivation of life as art became a protective strategy. The cultivation of 'significant' form, of pattern and design, enabled her to inhabit a world not far from that of the aesthetes of the 1890s. Her minutely controlled environment seems not unlike that created by Pater in his Oxford rooms, as he moved his lozenge-words across a table. For both writers, perhaps, the pursuit of the aesthetic in this way enabled them to feel that they had transcended the vulgar world of social and gender conflict. It was this belief which enabled them to write with such freedom across gender boundaries; and in Katherine Mansfield's case it enabled her to explore not just the range of her own sexuality (what she called in an early journal note 'the whole octave of sex') but also the bisexuality of her writing self and/or of writing itself, to pursue what Helene Cixous would call 'the other bisexuality'.[10]

To return to my beginning, the energy which Katherine Mansfield put into her life, both in the sense of the creation of the self-portrait of the letters and journals and the creation of the lived life as art, can clearly be related to her gender and to the difficult position of the woman writer in the early years of the century. But the crucial point about both these types of self-making was that Katherine Mansfield had a reasonable degree of control over the product. It was the breaking of this control which made her so angry when Constable misrepresented her qualities as a woman writer in the blurb for *Bliss* referred to in my opening quotation. Only too obviously, Katherine Mansfield has had no control over the re-presentations of her life which have taken place since her death. There is no space in this brief paper to do more than suggest some of the problems raised by the numerous re-presentations and re-creations of the 'life of Katherine Mansfield' published since 1923. The fictional portraits are perhaps among the most significant. She appeared in fictional form as Gudrun in *Women in Love,* endowed, perhaps surprisingly, with a fatal potency, and as the predatory Winnie in Francis Carco's *Les innocents,* first published in 1916. At the other end of the spectrum she appeared as the innocent 'Catherine' in William Orton's autobiographical novel *The Last Romantic* (1937). Such differences of interpretation are perhaps to be expected with a subject who had 'experimented' with life as she had done: all of these books were by men who, to some degree, had been sexually involved with her. Yet it is still depressing to recognize the fear which she inspired in these male colleagues/rivals, a fear which seems to have its source in the kind of 'reaction formation' against the power of the woman artist described by Gilbert and Gubar in *No Man's Land*.[11] It is particularly interesting to see the power of Katherine Mansfield's pen being transferred, as it were, to her female body: both Gudrun and Winnie are denied real status as artists but presented as sexually rapacious and for that reason fearsome.

The same fear seems to be latent in portraits of Katherine Mansfield in the letters and memoirs of many male contemporaries, for example Bertrand Russell and Lytton Strachey. Women such as Ottoline Morrell and, of course, Virginia Woolf, wrote of her with a good deal more sympathy. After her death, as is now well-known, Virginia Woolf wrote of her with generous insight, recognizing Katherine Mansfield's likeness and unlikeness to herself:

> Katherine has been dead a week, & how far am I obeying her 'do not quite forget Katherine' which I read in one of her old letters? Am I already forgetting her? It is strange to trace the progress of one's feelings. Nelly said in her sensational way at breakfast on Friday 'Mrs Murry's dead! It says so in the paper!' At that one feels — what? A shock of relief? — a rival the less? Then confusion at feel-

ing so little — then, gradually, blankness & disappointment; then a depression which I could not rouse myself from all that day. When I began to write, it seemed to me there was no point in writing. Katherine wont read it. Katherine's my rival no longer. More generously I felt. But though I can do this better than she could, where is she, who could do what I can't! [12]

Perhaps the phenomenon which would have raised Katherine Mansfield's worst suspicions would be not the presentation of her 'self' in the fiction and memoirs of contemporaries, but the numerous re-writings of her life in biographies written by people who had never known her. The cult of her life is perhaps most firmly established in France[13] but it is not confined to that country. For a writer who was so intensely aware of the ways in which a woman writer's life could be used to compromise her work, who tried so carefully to control the presentation of a life which she knew would be of interest to the public, the endless fascination which the 'life of Katherine Mansfield' seems to hold for those who did not know her might seem, to say the least, disquieting. Yet no writer can escape from biography, and were it not for the biographical accounts which have appeared, it would clearly have been impossible for me to have considered certain aspects of Katherine Mansfield's 'work', especially the 'lived life' as art. As my paper should suggest, as a feminist critic I think it is of the utmost importance that we should attempt to study aspects of both the 'life' and the 'art' of women artists, in order to breach the artificial barrier between 'life' and 'art' which has been set up by (professional) male critics and which, I think, contributes in a most insidious way to a devaluation of particular aspects of women's art. For cultural reasons, women have often had to find new and 'uncanonical' forms of artistic expression — including, in this particular case, aspects of the artist's life. While I am precisely *not* suggesting that we have to root through every woman artist's biography in order to appreciate her art, it may be that we have to interpret the boundaries of 'art' more flexibly if we are fully to appreciate the richness of women's creativity. As critics we do not need so much to 'think back through our mothers' in Virginia Woolf's rather abstract phrase, but, as Alice Walker more practically advises, we need to go 'in search of our mothers' gardens', in order to discover the variety of aspects of women's creativity and to celebrate in particular that interweaving of public and private worlds which informs and characterizes much of the work of women.

NOTES

1. Letter of 6 December 1920, in *Katherine Mansfield's Letters to John Middleton Murry. 1913-1922*, edited by J. Middleton Murry (London: Constable, 1951), p. 614.

2. 'Delicate' and 'touching' were terms used by D.H. Lawrence; 'sensitive' is of course V. Woolf's term in her review title 'A Terribly Sensitive Mind'.

3. Valerie Shaw, for example, in her comparatively recent *The Short Story: A Critical Introduction* (Essex: Longman, 1983) raises the issue of Katherine Mansfield's 'triviality' and inability to suggest the 'larger whole' (p. 132).

4. Virginia Woolf, *A Room of One's Own* (London: The Hogarth Press, 1929), pp. 110-111.

5. Sandra M. Gilbert and Susan Gubar, *No Man's Land: The Place of the Woman Writer in the Twentieth Century,* vol. 1, The War of the Words (New Haven and London: Yale University Press, 1988), ch. 1. They quote in passing Joyce's approving comment on Eliot's work: it 'ended the idea of poetry for ladies'. The remark has sexist implications despite the specificity of Joyce's target in a certain kind of gentility.

6. *Journal of Katherine Mansfield*, edited by John Middleton Murry, (London: Constable, 1954), p. 203.

7. Gillian Hanscombe and Virginia L. Smyers, *Writing for Their Lives*: *The Modernist Women 1910-1940* (London: The Women's Press, 1987), p. 5.

8. See Antony Alpers, *The Life of Katherine Mansfield* (London: Jonathan Cape, 1980), pp. 253-254.

9. *The Diary of Virginia Woolf, Vol. 2: 1920-1924*, edited by Anne Olivier Bell (London: The Hogarth Press, 1978), p. 226.

10. H. Cixous develops the idea of 'the other bisexuality' in *La jeune née* (1975) and 'Le rire de la méduse' (also 1975).

11. Op. cit., chs 1 and 5.

12. Op. cit., pp. 225-226.

13. It is still possible, I think, to see 'relics' in the public library in Menton, for example, a scarf, a lacquered box, etc.

Katherine Mansfield and Time

TANYA GRENFELL-WILLIAMS

In his essay 'Mansfield and the Orphans of Time', where Don Kleine discusses 'The Daughters of the Late Colonel', he argues that the story describes 'the daughters' last attempt to break free from [their father's] tyrannic use of time',[1] and regards it as 'Mansfield's outcry against a universe in which the clock is a masculine principle'.[2] Kleine's essay appears to be concerned with one aspect of time, that of linear or chronological time — as he states: 'the story's "now" is mired in history: a slow week in unlived lives' — but in section III of his essay he implies that 'profounder forces' have been thwarted. It is on this notion that I shall concentrate in this paper: I consider that these 'profounder forces' exist and are another aspect of time within the text. In fact this 'other' time 'The Daughters of the Late Colonel' offers us resembles what Julia Kristeva, the French theorist, has labelled 'women's time'.

Kristeva states that we confront two temporal dimensions: linear time, which she views as progression and arrival, which encompasses politics and history, and in which she posits language 'as the enunciation of a sequence of words';[3] secondly, cyclical time, which results from reproduction, gestation, biological rhythms and repetition. The implication of cyclical time is that of survival of the species, and it is connected, therefore, with eternity or 'monumental time'.[4] Kristeva argues that 'female subjectivity would seem to be linked both to cyclical time (repetition), and monumental time (eternity), conceptualizing time from the perspective of motherhood and reproduction'.[5]

In 'women's time' Kristeva's main preoccupation is with confronting this division in time by exploring women's differing approaches: firstly, women seeking equal rights; secondly, women seeking to remain outside the linear time of history and politics; thirdly, women reconciling maternal time with linear time.[6] My intention in using aspects of Kristeva's 'women's time' is thus to explore the 'profounder forces' that Kleine only tentatively suggests exist within the text of 'The Daughters of the Late Colonel', and to reveal the nature of Constantia and Josephine's relationship to this 'other' concept of time.

Kleine indicates at the beginning of his essay on 'the Daughters of the Late Colonel' that Katherine Mansfield has not followed a linear sequence, and he outlines the difference in pattern between the narrative sequence and the chronological sequence. In fact the narrative moves backwards and forwards from present to past and from past to present. This diffuse technique combined with that of the fluid movement through different perspectives — those of the daughters together, of their separate trains of thought and of the author's own comments — indicates the parameters of linear time yet suggests a move into an unbounded time. By using the technique of multiple perspectives rather than an omniscient commentary Katherine Mansfield avoids directing the reader towards a specific judgement of the protagonists. Through her use of 'indirect free style' the only obvious controlling force within the text is that of the father and all that he represents.

The late Colonel was part of that Anglo-Indian culture which was founded on the exploits of men, and its prescriptive values were an extension and extreme example of a patriarchal society. This closed male society extended its power not only over its females but also over the 'natives'. The daughters' experience of Anglo-India and of life in general was influenced by their father and his associates, and was now dependent upon communication with their male relations in England, such as Cyril, and by those still living in India, such as their brother Benny. Although there are still relics of the Indian experience around the house — such as the 'Indian carpet', the 'carved screen' and the 'Buddha' ornament on the mantelpiece — their father's Anglo-Indian background meant that he was cut off from Indian culture and from the Indian people. As Josephine indicates the family became even more isolated when he became estranged from his fellow Anglo-Indians:

> There had been father's Anglo-Indian friends before he quarrelled with them. But after that she and Constantia never met a single man except clergymen. (p. 401)

Because the daughters have lived their lives through their father and have been marginalized to the role of daughters of a colonel, they appear never to have been able to develop identities of their own. Instead they have been subjected to a patriarchal Anglo-Indian culture that is now being perpetuated by their brother.

Josephine raises the question 'If mother had lived, might they have married?'. Marriage to either an Anglo-Indian or a European would have meant the adoption of a certain culture, as well as a name, a family history, and possibly families of their own. Instead they remained economically and socially dependent upon their father, thereby having no particular status but that of dependent daughters. They appear to be suspended in linear time.

At one particular point in the story Josephine reflects on the absence of their mother, and I suggest that throughout the text there is an apparent lack of any obvious form of maternal nexus.

> Josephine remembered standing on a chair and pointing out that feather boa to Constantia and telling her that it was a snake that had killed their mother in Ceylon. . . . Would everything have been different if mother hadn't died? She didn't see why. (p. 401)

The absence of their mother meant that their lives had been dictated by their father and were spent 'looking after father and at the same time keeping out of father's way' (p. 401). The daughters' only link with any female tradition appears to be dependent upon their memories of their mother and upon the aunt who looked after them until they left school; even Hilda was an 'unknown sister-in-law'. Dominated by their father there was never any opportunity for their sexual difference to express itself.

However, Katherine Mansfield offers the reader an insight into something deeper, what Kleine calls 'profounder forces', and what I suggest could be 'women's time'. We are warned of 'something' secret when Constantia

> walked over to the mantelpiece to her favourite Buddha. And the stone and gilt image, whose smile always gave her such a queer feeling, almost a pain and yet a pleasant pain, seemed to-day to be more than smiling. He knew something; he had a secret. 'I know something that you don't know,' said her Buddha. Oh, what was it, what could it be? And yet she had always felt there was . . . something. (p. 401)

Through religious connections Katherine Mansfield has created the feeling of mysticism, hidden meanings, the unknown. The Buddhist faith at once evokes the notion of reincarnation, rebirth and thus repetition; it can therefore be related to Kristeva's 'cyclical time'. Moreover there are further religious connotations in the story that confirm this interpretation: the reference to the snake, a phallic image, is a clear allusion to the Bible, and the Adam and Eve myth where the snake is the agent of Eve's downfall and mankind's mortality. Death in itself is linked to linear time as it puts a restriction on time by marking the end of a phase. The consequence of this is the need for reproduction to ensure the survival of the species with its biological rhythms, sex, life, death and repetition, which again reinforces the notion of 'cyclical time'.

These religious references point to 'women's time' and precede a further indication of what the 'something' could be:

> [Constantia] remembered the times she had come in here, crept out of bed in her nightgown when the moon was full, and lain on the floor with her arms outstretched, as though she was crucified. (p. 402)

Here, once more, Biblical allusions are used. Yet Constantia considers what urged her to lie on the floor in such an attitude:

> Why? The big, pale moon had made her do it. The horrid dancing figures on the carved screen had leered at her and she hadn't minded. She remembered too how, whenever they were at the seaside, she had gone off by herself and got as close to the sea as she could, and sung something, something she had made up, while she gazed all over the restless water. There had been this other life . . . But it all seemed to have happened in a kind of tunnel. It wasn't real. It was only when she came out of the tunnel into the moonlight or by the sea or into a thunderstorm that she really felt herself. (p. 402)

Apart from another life, or perhaps an 'other' time, this suggests that a certain mesmeric power was emitted by the moon. This idea can also be found in a *Journal* entry dated October 1920:

> Suddenly through the kitchen window I saw the moon. It was so marvellously beautiful that I walked out of the kitchen door, through the garden and leaned over the gate before I knew what I was doing. The moon was full, transparent, glittering. It hung over the sighing sea. I looked at it for a long time. [7]

Both quotations suggest a mystical experience, a movement from one life or space to another. I consider that there is a movement towards what could be defined as a 'feminine' space. The words 'pale moon', 'moonlight', and 'water' are suggestive of 'feminine' imagery. The notion of the 'feminine' is reinforced through reference to the 'emitting' moon which contrasts with that of the 'thieving sun' that shines across the Indian carpet and fades the photograph of their mother. Andrew Gurr and Clare Hanson argue that 'Josephine, the more "practical and sensible" of the sisters, is the sun and Constantia is moon'.[8] In my opinion the 'thieving sun' represents the Colonel, who also takes rather than gives. The sun was once employed as a means to measure linear time, whilst the moon, with its associations with the full moon, its monthly cycles and tides, suggests fluidity, repetition, rhythms and cycles, and tends to draw out the 'profounder forces' or the more mystical, 'feminine' side. As Katherine Mansfield states in her *Journal,* 'it wasn't for nothing Constantia chose the moon and water for instance!'.[9]

In 'Prelude', Linda Burnell, like Katherine Mansfield and the Colonel's daughters, is also drawn to the moon. In section VII we are told:

> It was quite dark outside now and heavy dew was falling. When Linda shut the window the cold dew touched her finger tips. Far away a dog barked. 'I believe there is going to be a moon,' she said.
>
> At the words, and with the cold wet dew on her fingers, she felt as though the moon had risen — that she was being strangely discovered in a flood of cold light. (p. 243)

Linda then moves and sits by her husband Stanley, resuming her place as his wife and as a mother, and aligning herself with her own mother. In contrast to the Colonel's daughters, Linda appears to understand her 'moonlight' experience. But, then, she lives with her mother, Mrs Fairfield, and enjoys a close filial relationship with her. As Linda puts it, 'there was something comforting in the sight of her [mother] that she could never do without'(p. 238).

Linda and Mrs Fairfield both ponder the significance of the aloe, a plant which is said to flower 'once every hundred years'. This extends the notion of reproductive time outside the limited span of our human life. In this story the moonlight and the aloe combine to provide an image of female sexuality. Whilst Linda examines her own life, her mother walks silently alongside her. Mrs Fairfield is firmly located in 'women's time' because of her creative, nurturing, maternal capacity. Time for her is unbounded and yet exists in seasons or cycles; she regards the autumn as that time of year when everything

Agave, Bothanical Gardens, Tinakori Road Wellington

should be productive, swollen, ripe and in a state of fruitfulness. This is highlighted by her reply, when Linda asks her what she has been thinking about:

> I wondered as we passed the orchard what the fruit trees were like and whether we should be able to make much jam this autumn. There are splendid healthy currant bushes in the vegetable garden. (p. 255)

The division of time into 'women's time' and 'linear time' is not only evident in these texts but pervades much of Katherine Mansfield's writing. At the beginning of 'At the Bay' we are told that as the sun had not risen 'there was nothing to mark which was beach and where was the sea' (p. 441). The sun appears to impose limitations on the scenery as its presence does on the lives of Constantia and Josephine. Stanley Burnell, we are told in 'Prelude', does his morning exercises 'standing firm in the exact centre of a square of sunlight' (p. 233); in 'At the Bay', he insists he has only 'twenty-five minutes' before he leaves for work, then later, clock-watching, reminds his family that he has 'only twelve and a half minutes before the coach passes' (p. 445). Burnell is clearly hounded by time. In 'The Voyage' the sign above the grandfather's bed stresses the urgency of time. It reads:

Lost! One Golden Hour
Set with Sixty Diamond Minutes.
No *Reward Is Offered*
For It Is GONE FOR EVER! (p. 476)

Katherine Mansfield too shared this feeling, for in her journal entry of 17 January 1922 she stated : 'I am pursued by time myself'.[10]

Stanley's insistence on time can be compared with Jonathan Trout's concern for his brief existence also expressed in 'At the Bay'. The story takes place on a single day moving from morning to night, yet throughout there are significant references to life and death. Trout contemplates life when he comments that:

> all the while I'm thinking, like that moth, or that butterfly, or whatever it is, 'The shortness of life! The shortness of life!' I've only one night or one day, and there's this vast dangerous garden, waiting out there, undiscovered, unexplored. (p. 464)

In contrast however, Linda Burnell 'dreamed [her] morning away'. She is positioned between her mother and Beryl, her spinster sister. Indeed her gradual awareness of her own female subjectivity — presented in her relationship with her son and developed through her conceptualization of time from the perspective of motherhood and reproduction — moves her further away from Beryl and closer towards her mother.

The reader is also confronted with the experience of time as eternity when Kezia insists that her grandmother must not die. Mrs Fairfield reflects upon and judges the past, whilst face to face with the future, in the form of her grand-daughter Kezia.

> It was the old woman's turn to consider. Did it make her sad? To look back, back. To stare down the years, as Kezia had seen her doing. To look after *them* as a woman does, long after *they* were out of sight. Did it make her sad? No, life was like that. (p. 456)

In considering Josephine and Constantia's relationship to 'women's time' in the light of that of Linda and Mrs Fairfield's, it could be argued that because the sisters are unmarried and childless they, like Beryl Fairfield and Katherine Mansfield herself, are outside 'monumental time'. It would seem that marriage is the agency that brings 'monumental time' to women. However, because their father is dead, and death is linked to linear time, both daughters attempt to escape death by trying to move into another space. They attempt to suspend time, but cannot maintain this suspended state and, as Katherine Mansfield says in her letter to William Gerhardi, 'after that, it [seems] to me, they died as surely as their father was dead'.[11]

NOTES

1. Don W. Kleine, 'Mansfield and the Orphans of Time', *Modern Fiction Studies* 24 (1973), p. 430.

2. Ibid., p. 431.

3. *The Kristeva Reader*, edited by T. Moi (Basil Blackwell, 1986), p. 187.

4. Ibid., p. 191.

5. Ibid., p. 187.

6. Ibid., pp. 188-211.

7. *Journal of Katherine Mansfield* 1904-1922, edited by J. Middleton Murry (London: Constable, 1954), pp. 219-220.

8. Clare Hanson, Andrew Gurr, *Katherine Mansfield* (New York: St. Martin's Press, 1981), p. 92.

9. *Journal of Katherine Mansfield,* p. 281.

10. Katherine Mansfield, *Letters and Journals*, edited by C. K. Stead (Harmondsworth: Penguin, 1977), p. 251.

11. Ibid., p. 224.

Frau Brechenmacher and Stanley Burnell: Some Background Discussion on the Treatment of the Roles of Men and Women in the Writing of Katherine Mansfield

GILLIAN BODDY

In recent years Katherine Mansfield has rightly, if belatedly, received considerable critical attention as an early feminist writer. In this paper I would like to provide some biographical background to the exploration of the roles of men and women, bearing in mind her comment in 1922 to the South African writer, Sarah Gertrude Millin: 'I think the only way to live as a writer is to draw upon one's familiar life. The life we return to over and over again, the "do you remember" life is always the past. And the curious thing is that if we describe that which seems to us so intensely personal, other people take it to themselves and understand it as if it were their own'.[1] She grew up at a time when the roles of women were being re-assessed, so creating what her friend D.H. Lawrence called 'THE problem of today'. Her stories explore a wide range of roles and relationships; her letters and journals reveal ideas and views which are sometimes contradictory. A study of these roles and relationships reveals perception, anger, compassion and, at times, humour.

In 1895 Mrs Roy Devereux wrote, 'Life has taken on a strange unloveliness and the least beautiful thing therin is the New Woman'.[2] In the 1880's and 1890's New Zealand women, like their sisters in Britain, agitated for equality and the right to vote. The Suffrage Bill was, in fact, passed in September 1893 but, as so often happens, legislation did little to alter public attitudes. The lives of most women changed very little and so the struggle for true equality continued.

In 1897 Kathleen Beauchamp's uncle, Frank Dyer, married Phoebe Seddon, the Premier's daughter and the first member of the Women's Social and Political League to marry. With the usual coy tone deemed appropriate for such events, *The New Zealand Mail* described the occasion at which the members presented Miss Seddon with her wedding present: a 'handsome hall stand' duly inscribed, and an autograph album. The League members believed it would be prized because 'it had come from ... a society which had done so much good work in the Liberal cause, and also in the matter of obtaining those rights which are being gradually conceded to women. The presentation was one more step in the advance, for this, Mrs Mason believed, was the first occasion on which an organisation of women having a political creed had made a presentation to one of its members on such an occasion .... It was also the first time in the annals of this Colony that the daughter of a Premier had entered into the bonds of matrimony while her father held that 'important position'.[3] It is interesting too to note that the bride's veil with its silk-embroidered lilies of the valley was also given and embroidered by the League. Radical feminists they were not!

In her reply Miss Seddon mentioned that 'The present she had received was a sensible one, just what she would expect from such a body of women.... Hers was the first marriage out of the League and she could do no better than advise the younger members to follow in her footsteps. Although she was going to be married she did not intend to give up the League – (applause) – that was one condition she had already made. (Laughter)'.

But it would seem that even having a family member who belonged to 'an organisation of women having a political creed' effected little change in the Beauchamp household, which although predominantly a house of women was very much dominated by Stanley Beauchamp, the family 'pa-man'. Many Wellingtonians in fact would still have agreed with one citizen who had publicly displayed posters advising electioneering women to go home, to look after their children, cook their husband's dinners, empty the slops and generally attend to the domestic affairs for which Nature designed them. 'By taking this advice they will gain the respect of all right-minded people – an end not to be attained by unsexing themselves'[4].

Katherine Mansfield grew up against such a background and it was her denunciation of such traditional views that first attracted me in Wellington in the 1960's, before the heady days of the women's movement and Germaine Greer's first visit. Now rightly regarded as a feminist, though one who used her writing rather than political groups to express her views, Katherine Mansfield seems at first to have been unsympathetic to the kind of organisation to which her aunt belonged, and she always used the term feminist rather disparagingly.

Probably late in 1903, Kathleen Beauchamp wrote a sketch beginning "I am afraid I must be very old-fashioned. I used to pride myself upon being quite a modern woman, but within the last week I have had a rude awakening". The young female narrator and her husband receive an invitation, bedecked with floral wreaths and angels blowing trumpets, to a 'Lecture on Physical Culture by Miss Mickle at the Assembly Rooms'. She continues with a lively, satirical description of the women, 'Great tall gaunt looking figures, and all angles. They seemed to be seized with a mania to appear masculine. Men's books, men's gloves, men's hats.... They had a hungry look in their eyes. I longed to take them home and show them my babies....' Miss Mickle is an object of even greater derision. 'It seemed to be her great desire to squeeze out all the tenderness, all the loving, all the affectionate ways that should belong by rights to every woman, and to put in their places divided skirts and no figures'.[5]

To what degree this reflected Kathleen Beauchamp's own views I cannot guess, but by the time she returned from London at the end of 1906 her views were, thankfully, very different, although even then there were moments of ambivalence. Not only had she become a follower of Oscar Wilde and Pater, but she had discovered Marie Bashkirtseff, the young Russian painter, sculptor and musician who had died in her early 20's. *Le Journal de Marie Bashkirtseff* (1877) had been translated into English by Mathilde Blind in 1889. Not only do this young painter's self portraits have a strong visual resemblance to some photographs of Katherine Mansfield, but sections of her journal must have seemed to Katherine Mansfield to reflect her own views, enforced as she was to return to a 'land of Philistines' where people had not yet 'learned their alphabet'. 'We live but once and my time is being wasted in the most unworthy fashion' wrote Bashkirtseff, talking of her attempts to establish herself as a painter in Paris. Bashkirtseff commented, 'These gentlemen despise us, and it is only when they come across a powerful, even brutal piece of work, that they are satisfied.... It is the work of a young man, they said of mine'. To the young K.M. who had decided already to escape to London and freedom, and to be 'an author', Bashkirtseff's words must have seemed a credo, 'What I long for is the freedom of going about alone, of coming and going... that's the freedom without which one cannot become a great artist'.

Wellington's colonial society was not one to encourage such views. Her life became a dual existence. On the one hand she went through the social rounds which were deemed to be a 'Suitable Appropriate Existence' with some success and even, apparently, enjoyment. She considered herself to have been engaged to several young men and advised her sister that she was greatly in demand at dances. The newspapers of the time, in columns such as 'Tea Table Topics', report with infinite detail on the minutiae of the Beauchamp's social existence: what Miss K. Beauchamp wore; the balls, afternoon teas, at-homes and bridge parties she attended. It is little wonder that in her fiction the descriptions of clothes and hats are so detailed. Think of the significance of the 'black hat' in 'The Garden Party' and Beryl's fantasy costume in 'At the Bay'. Such things were clearly of much importance in the Edwardian capital where her family had gradually acquired considerable status and prestige. As she dryly remarked in 'Juliet', 'the days full of perpetual Society functions, the hours full of clothes discussions, the waste of life... the days, weeks, months, years of it all. Her father, with his successful characteristic respectable face, crying "Now's the time. What have I got for my money? Come along now, deck yourself out show the world that you are expensive"'.[6] Yet it's not surprising, despite this satirical view, that for the rest of her life discussion of clothes featured frequently in her letters to her family and friends, and her notebook entries reveal lists of clothes for weekends away, all carefully colour co-ordinated, even in the last weeks of her life.

Yet there was also a secret life in which she poured out her longings for London and new experiences into 'huge complaining' diaries, many of which she later destroyed. There was time too for her intimate relationship with Edie Bendall, with whom she walked on the Tinakori Hills and spent weekends at the little cottage across the harbour. Unconventional too was her relationship with Maata Mahupuku, a beautiful Maori princess with whom she had been at school in Wellington and met again in London. Maata was one of the guests at Chaddie Beauchamp's birthday ball in 1907, decorously dressed in ivory silk and Valencienne lace. K.M.'s notebooks speak of an intense, confusing and complicated relationship.

K.M. may have been influenced by the new and exciting ideas of Wilde and Bashkirtseff but Wellington society remained rigidly conventional and she carried those impressions with her for the rest of her life. We can only imagine her response to the attitudes expressed in *The New Zealand Mail*, when reporting on the Women's Suffrage movement in July 1907, it denounced it as 'bad for the woman, bad for the little ones... and bad for the nation'.[7] A little later it warned 'The so-called new woman is an utter failure... the sort of woman that people call intelligent is the most awful nuisance in the world... she combines the respectful dullness of a Church meeting with the mental fatigue of a mathematical problem... *Moral:* bear in mind men like to be amused and *never* instructed'.[8]

Some of her very early fiction continued in fact to reflect a very traditional view in her treatment of male and female roles, for example the unfinished novel, 'Juliet', begun in London and 'The Education of Audrey'. Written in Wellington in January 1908 it is a rather curious, exaggerated piece set in Wellington's Day's Bay and London. The heroine breathlessly capitulates in the last lines of somewhat purple prose:

> "Ah, there are heights and depths in Art and Life that you have never dreamed of Audrey.... You are playing on the outskrits of a forest filled with beautiful scarlet flowers. One day, sooner or later, if you want to fulfil your destiny, someone will take you by the hand and lead you there, and you will learn".
> Silence again in the dark room ... the silver rain beat against the windows.
> She suddenly turned towards him and stretched out her hands – "Teach me, Max" said Audrey. (p. 16)

Only five months later, however, the nineteen year old Katherine Mansfield wrote enthusiastically to her sister, Vera, 'All this suffragist movement is *excellent* for our sex – kicked policemen or not kicked policemen'[9] and confided to her journal,

> I feel that I do now realise, dimly, what women in the future will be capable of. They truly, as yet, have never had their chance. Talk of our enlightened days and our emancipated country – pure nonsense. We are firmly held in the self-fashioned chains of slavery. Yes — now I see that they are self-fashioned and must be self-removed ... here then is a little summary of what I need – power, wealth and freedom. It is the hopelessly insipid doctrine that love is the only thing in the world, taught, hammered into women, from generation to generation, which hampers us so cruelly. We must get rid of that bogey – and then, then comes the opportunity of happiness and freedom.[10]

In 1908, shortly after her return to England to find Life with a capital L, Katherine Mansfield remarked to her lover, Garnet Trowell, 'I could not be a suffragette – the world was too full of laughter. Oh, I feel that I could remedy the evils of this world so much more easily – don't you?'[11] In spite of this denial, a few years later when Emily Davidson became a martyr to the suffragette cause by throwing herself under the King's horse, Katherine Mansfield defended her vociferously. The ensuing incident was described with delight by Edward Marsh to the poet Rupert Brooke:

> She really ought to remember she's a lady. The provocation was that the woman said that all suffragettes ought to be trampled to death by horses. Katherine, tho' not a suffragette protested and the woman said, 'you with your painted lips![12]

Her way of remedying the evils of the world, her 'cry against corruption', was, of course, her fiction. In her writing she disproved the long held attitude so neatly summarised by her friend, Virginia Woolf: 'This is an important book ... because it deals with war. This is an insignificant book because it deals with the feelings of women in the drawing room.'[13] Although she was later to mock some aspects of the 'New Woman' of her time, Katherine Mansfield was in many ways resentful and angry at many aspects of the traditional female role. But throwing off the chains which would bind her to that role was not always as simple as she had envisaged. She explained in a letter to Murry in 1913:

> When I have to clean up twice over or wash up extra unnecessary things I get frightfully impatient and want to be working. So often, this week, I've heard you and Gordon talking while I washed dishes. Well, somone's got to wash dishes get food. Otherwise – "there's nothing in the house but eggs to eat". Yes. I hate hate HATE doing these things that you accept just as all men accept of their women. I can only play the servant with very bad grace indeed. Its all very well for females who have nothing else to do ... & then you say I am a tyrant & wonder because I get tired at night! ... I loathe myself, today. I detest this woman who "superintends" you and rushes about, slamming doors & slooping water – all untidy with her blouse out and her nails grimed. I am disgusted and repelled by the creature who shouts at you "you might at least empty the pail and wash out the tea leaves!" Yes, no wonder you "come over silent".[14]

At the end of the following year Katherine Mansfield found the same solution to these domestic chores that her mother had always enjoyed, describing to her mother 'I have engaged a pleasant decent body to come and do the strenuous work... I mean the *scrubbing,* my dear, and lighting fires, cleaning stove etc. Scrubbing when one runs it to earth really doesn't seem to me to be a human occupation at all. I'd rather keep the floor moist and grow a crop of grass on it'.[15] Her stories frequently show women in the two roles of privileged employer and domestic employee, drawn from the Mansfield-Murry and Beauchamp menages. Who can forget Alice of 'Prelude' and 'At the Bay'? Katherine Mansfield confessed that she was a failure at 'domestic virtues' being 'no good at buttons, puddings', although her letters and journals do, in fact, contain recipes! She admitted too that 'knitting turns me into an imbecile. It's the female tradition I suppose'.

But the female tradition frequently provoked anger in her stories, not humour. 'The Woman at the Store' was once a barmaid 'pretty as a waxdoll' who 'knew one hundred and twenty-five different ways of kissing'. After six years of marriage and four miscarriages she has become a pathetic figure. Her front teeth were knocked out and she had red pulpy hands. "'I says to 'im, I says, what do you think I'm doin' up 'ere... Over and over I tells 'im – you've broken my spirit, and spoiled my looks, and wot for.... I 'ear them two words knockin' inside me all the time — "Wot for!"'(pp. 114 - 115). Her cry ehoes that of little Frau Brechenmacher in a powerful story based partly on Katherine Mansfield's observations of life in Bad Wörishofen where, alone and ill, she miscarried. Sent by her officious, chauvinistic husband to dress in the dark passages so he may preen himself in the light of the kitchen, Frau Brechenmacher, then follows him to the Gasthaus where Herr Brechenmacher completely overawed by this grand manner, so far forgot his rights as a husband as to beg his wife's pardon for jostling her against the banisters in his efforts to get ahead of everybody else.

> At the head of the centre table sat the bride and bridegroom, she in a white dress trimmed with stripes and bows of coloured ribbon, giving her the appearance of an iced cake all ready to be cut and served in neat little pieces to the bridegroom beside her, who wore a suit of white clothes much too large for him. (pp. 44 - 45)

After the festivities

> They walked home in silence. Herr Brechenmacher strode ahead, she stumbled after him. White and forsaken lay the road from the railway station to their house – a cold rush of wind blew her hood from her face,

and suddenly she remembered how they had come home together the first night. Now they had five babies and twice as much money; *but* – "Na, what is it all for?" she muttered. (p. 47)

The story ends bleakly

"Always the same", she said – 'all over the world the same; but, God in heaven – but *stupid*'
Then even the memory of the wedding faded quite. She lay down on the bed and put her arm across her face like a child who expected to be hurt as Herr Brechenmacher lurched in. (p. 48)

Often the women in her stories are alone, vulnerable, 'les dames seules', relatively unwary and naive and frequently propositioned by predatory men. Sabina in 'At Lehmann's' for example, intrigued and puzzled, finds herself laughing with the Young Man who has shown her a pornographic postcard:

Laughter ceased. She looked up at him once, then down at the floor, and began breathing like a frightened little animal.
He pulled her closer still and kissed her mouth.
"Na, what are you doing?" she whispered.
He let go her hands, he placed his on her breasts, and the room seemed to swim round Sabrina.

Many of her stories are told by a young female narrator who has little trouble gaining our sympathy. Several, however, are narrated by men, some of them thoroughly unlikeable. Any one who dismisses her stories, as H.E. Bates does, as being peopled only by 'chattering overgrown schoolgirls busy asking and answering breathless facile questions about love, life and happiness'[16] need only sit down for half an hour with 'A Married Man's Story' and 'The Man Without a Temperament'. The best known man in Katherine Mansfield's stories is probably Stanley Burnell who appears in 'Prelude' and 'At the Bay' and is the prototype of many other characters – the stern father who applies corporal punushment in 'The Little Girl', Andreas Binzer who longs for a son and heir in 'A Birthday' but is concerned only with his own sensitivity as his wife endures childbirth, the Boss in 'The Fly' who 'had arranged to weep' but 'no tears came'. Much of Stanley is, inevitably, drawn from Katherine Mansfield's own father, the successful 'pa-man' Harold Beauchamp. Fit, energetic, ambitious, he delights in his 'firm, obedient body', his 'amazing vigour'. In 'Prelude', that story which encompasses the life span of woman in only forty pages, Linda, his wife, finds his passionate embraces threatening. 'He was too strong for her, she had always hated things that rush at her, from a child. There were times when he was frightening'.

Stanley is paternalistic, self-centred and clumsy in his heartiness: a man who expected his sugar spooned into his tea, his slippers put out for him each night, he is the epitome of all that Katherine Mansfield despised and rejected. Yet there is also compassion in her portrait of him, showing that she understood him after all. Even in 1915, when there was still so much that was unresolved between her and her father, she wrote in 'The Apple Tree'

> father was a self made man and the price he had to pay for everything was so huge and so painful that nothing rang so sweet to him as to hear his purchase praised. He was young and sensitive still... He still had hours when he walked up and down in the moonlight half deciding to check this confounded rushing to the office every day.

Linda herself reveals this understanding of Stanley in 'At the Bay':

> Well, she was married to him. And what was more she loved him. Not the Stanley whom every one saw, not the everyday one; but a timid, sensitive, innocent Stanley who knelt down every night to say his prayers.
> But the trouble was – here Linda felt almost inclined to laugh, though heaven knows it was no laughing matter – she saw her Stanley so seldom. There were glimpses, moments, breathing spaces of calm, but all the rest of the time it was like living in a house that couldn't be cured of the habit of catching fire, or a ship that got wrecked every day. And it was always Stanley who was in the thick of the danger. Her whole time was spent in rescuing him, and restoring him, and calming him down, and listening to his story. And what was left of her time was spent in the dread of having children.
> ...
> Yes, that was her real grudge against life; that was what she could not understand. That was the question she asked and asked, and listened in vain for the answer. It was all very well to say it was the common lot of women to bear children. It wasn't true. She, for one, could prove that wrong. She was broken, made weak, her courage was gone, through child-bearing. (pp. 229 - 230)

And there is the crux of so much of Katherine Mansfield's writing – 'the common lot of women to bear children. It wasn't true'.

Time and time again she attacks the commonly held views of women as child-bearing chattels, useless if they were too old to bear children or had no money or property to lure men into marriage. Some, like Ada Moss in 'Pictures', Miss Brill and Ma Parker, are older, alone in a society that places no value on them. 'The Daughters of the Late Colonel', the only story which really pleased her, is also an indictment of the patriarchal system. Bullied for so long by their apoplectic, domineering, paternalistic father, they can no longer even decide whether to have fish 'fried' or 'boiled'. They are like the 'terrified blancmange', reduced to unassertive indecison even by their employees. It is interesting to glance for a moment at Katherine Mansfield's own explanation of the genesis of those sisters: 'You see the Daughters of the Late Colonel were a mixture of Miss Edith, Miss Emily, Ida, Sylvia Payne, Lizzie Fleg, and "Cyril" was based on Chummie. To write stories one has to go back into the past. And it's as though we took a flower from all kinds of gardens to make a new bouquet'.[17]

Women were also depicted as caught by the conventional double standard in sexual morality, as is clearly shown in 'This Flower', surely a diagnosis of a pregnancy. This too must have been triggered off by that 'do you remember life'. When she began writing it she was alone and unhappy in Italy, 'going over all the old life before the baby of Garnet's love'.[18] And in that cataloguing of her past the memory of the abortion in 1911 to which Ida Baker and Beatrice Hastings referred, although doubted by some biographers, must also have found its place.

She resented too the financial dependence of women. Think of the wife and husband in 'Six Years After'. Again he is blue-eyed and energetic but this time, surprisingly, he is briefly and wryly aware of his own self-absorption and gratification which he then conveniently dismisses as 'a law of marriage'! She is waiting for him to tip the ship's steward, 'she did hope he would be tipped adequately. It was on occasions like this (and her life seemed to be full of such occasions) that she wished it was the woman who controlled the purse.' (p. 506)

Often, and not surprisingly therefore, the worlds of male and female seem only tenuously linked. The men seem quite alien at times to that world in which women are comfortable. It was not just a question of her own bisexuality – most of the women in her stories are simply warmly affectionate and often share an underlying complicity – a sense of 'You and I against the world'. In her early notebook story 'Juliet' she had written of the friendship between Pearl and Juliet:

> "Our friendship is unique... All the comforts of matrimony with none of its encumbrances... we are both individuals. We both ask from the other personal privacy, and we can be silent for hours when the desire seizes us!... Think of a man always with you. A woman cannot be wholly natural with a man – there is always a feeling that she must take care that she doesn't let him go".[19]

This sense of collusion between women in some other fiction is not surprising when we consider how important her many relationships with women were to K.M. herself. It was so often from them, that she gained the nurturing and affection she needed and felt she had been denied by her mother.

At times the male and female characters do achieve a kind of closeness and understanding, though it is rarely sexual but more akin to the kind of sympathetic bonding that links the women in her stories. More often, though, the men are shown to be too inarticulate, too uncommunicative and too unevolved for this intimacy to take place. Often too a propensity for violence, cruelty and coarseness is suggested. Some, however, win our liking and sympathy, and at times she shows with great clarity and subtlety the physical chemistry that attracts men and women. Something of the same tension is also found between Bertha Young and Pearl Fulton, and sensed by Beryl in relation to Mrs. Kember in 'At the Bay'.

Although some of the male characters are truly detestable – Harry Kember, Harry Young, Raoul Duquette, Mr. Reginald Peacock are a few examples – Katherine Mansfield's sympathies are not always with her women characters. In 'At the Bay' Jonathan Trout is shown as an atypical male. He is more articulate than Stanley, willing to talk about 'cranky' ideas and dreams; happier talking in the garden than sitting in his jail of an office. Through him Katherine Mansfield gives a picture of what men might be, if only they were allowed to be, and had the courage to break free from the role society has traditionally imposed on them.

> "It seems to me just as imbecile, just as infernal, to have to go to the office on Monday", said Jonathan, "as it always has done and always will do. To spend all the best years of one's life sitting on a stool from

nine to five, scratching in somebody's ledger! It's like an insect that's flown into a room of its own accord. I dash against the walls, dash against the windows, flop against the ceiling, do everything on God's earth, in fact, except fly out again. And all the while I'm thinking...'The shortness of life.' I've only one night or one day, and there's this vast dangerous garden, waiting out there, undiscovered, unexplored". (pp. 231 - 232)

Consider too William in 'Marriage à la Mode', the long-suffering husband in 'The Escape'. Particularly interesting too are 'Late Spring' and 'This Flower'. In 'This Flower' we empathise with the young woman who seems caught in a kind of male conspiracy between the doctor and her lover; in the unpublished version of 'Late Spring', however, the perspective shifts; it is the doctor who surprisingly gains our sympathy.

It is one of the characteristics of Katherine Mansfield's writing that she works through suggestion, implication, 'half tones'. She does not need to denounce so many of the male characters who inhabit her fiction as patriarchal, arrogant, chauvinistic. They betray themselves, usually unwittingly, through their actions and words.

Many adolescent readers of today's modern romances would identify with Beryl's fantasies in 'Prelude' and 'At the Bay'. But they should ready warily! Beryl – who is drawn partly from Katherine Mansfield's Aunt Belle and partly from the adolescent Mansfield herself, yearns for romance in 'Prelude':

The window was wide open; it was warm, and somewhere out there in the garden a young man, dark and slender, with mocking eyes, tiptoed among the bushes, and gathered the flowers into a big bouquet, and slipped under her window and held it up to her. She saw herself bending forward. He thrust his head among the bright waxy flowers, sly and laughing...
...
A young man, immensely rich, has just arrived from England. He meets her quite by chance... The new governor is unmarried. ... There is a ball at Government House. ... Who is that exquisite creature in eau-de-nil satin? Beryl Fairfield...'

But the next paragraph begins, "'The thing that pleases me," said Stanley, leaning against the side of the bed and giving himself a good scratch on his shoulders and back before turning in, "is that I've got the place dead cheap, Linda!"' As so often in her work, illusion is dissipated by reality. the mere juxtaposition of the two is enough.

Nevertheless, towards the end of her life, Katherine Mansfield wrote:

> What is happening to "married pairs?' They are almost extinct. I confess, for my part, I believe in marriage. It seems to me the only possible relation that really is satisfying. And how else is one to have peace of mind to enjoy life and to do one's work? Does this sound hopelessly old-fashioned? I suppose it does. But there it is. To make jam with Jack, to look for flowers, to talk, to grow things, even to watch Jack darning his socks over a lemon seems to me to take up all the time one isn't working. People nowadays seem to live in such confusion. I have a horror of dark muddles.

She went so far as to criticise contemporary women writers for their new permissiveness:

> a book for a rubber shop (mes excuses!)... Female writers discovering a freedom, a frankness, a license to speak their hearts, reveal themselves as... sex maniacs. There's not a relationship between a man & woman that isn't the one sexual relationship – at its lowest. Intimacy is the sexual act.

These may seem surprising comments from a woman whose own life had frequently defied the sexual and social mores of conventional society but Katherine Mansfield seems to have examined her own behaviour 'confronted myself as it were... It wasn't flattering or pleasant or easy'. Relationships for her, in both her writing and her life, were now to be achieved through a very different kind of intimacy. The sexual act alone was not enough. The traditional, time-honoured relations of the domineering paternalistic male and dependent, financially-insecure submissive woman was no longer valid, if indeed it ever had been.

Clearly equality between loving individuals was the ideal basis for a relationship. And so two months before her death she wrote to her husband from Fontainebleau: 'You are you. I am I. We can only lead our own lives together'.

NOTES

1. To Sarah Gertrude Millin, March, 1922.

2. R. Devereux ('A Woman of the Day') 'The Feminine Potential', *Saturday Review* 22 June, 1895, pp. 824-25.

3. The New Zealand Mail, 14 January, 1897.

4. Poster issued by Henty Wright, Mein Street, Wellington, Alexander Turnbull Library.

5. Notebook 37, Alexander Turnbull Library, qMS (1240).

6. 'Juliet' Notebook 1, Alexander Turnbull Library, qMS (1242).

7. *The New Zealand Mail,* 31 July, 1907.

8. *The New Zealand Mail,* 20 September, 1907.

9. To Vera Beauchamp, 12 June, 1908. *The Collected Letters of Katherine Mansfield,* eds. Vincent O'Sullivan and Margaret Scott, (Oxford: Claredon Press, 1984), Vol.1, p. 47.

10. Notebook 39, May 1908, Katherine Mansfield Papers, Alexander Turnbull Library, qMS (1243).

11. To Garnet Trowell, 17 September 1908, *The Collected Letters of Katherine Mansfield,* eds., Vincent O'Sullivan & Margaret Scott Vol 1 p 60.

12. Christopher Hassall, *Edward Marsh* (London: Longman, 1959), p. 226.

13. Virginia Woolf, *A Room of One's Own* (London: Granada, 1983), p.70.

14. To J. Middleton Murry, May - June, 1913. *Collected Letters,* eds., O'Sullivan and Scott, Vol. 1, p. 125.

15. To Annie Beauchamp, 15 December, 1914, ibid, p. 144.

16. H.E. Bates, *The Modern Short Story* (London: Michael Joseph, 1971), pp. 129-130.

17. To Vera Mackintosh Bell, March 1922. Katherine Mansfield Papers, Newberry Library.

18. 12 January, 1920. Katherine Mansfield Papers, 119/45 Alexander Turnbull Library.

19. 'Juliet' Notebook 1, Alexander Turnbull Library, qMS (1240).

20. To Sylvia Lynd, 24 September, 1921. *The Letters of Katherine Mansfield* ed. J.M. Murry (London: Constable, 1928), p. 138.

21. To J.M. Murry, 17 October, 1920. *Katherine Mansfield's Letters to John Middleton Murry* (London: Constable, 1951), p. 565.

22. Ibid, 7 November, 1922, p. 685.

NARRATIVE STRATEGIES

Irony in the Short Stories of Katherine Mansfield

IRÈNE SIMON

It is perhaps unfair to have chosen irony as the topic of this paper since the stories of Katherine Mansfield we remember best, those which, according to general critical opinion as well as to her own assessment, are her best, are not, on the whole, ones in which the author's stance is ironical. Yet we should remember that not all her stories sprang from her love of life or were meant to recreate what she came to regard as the lost paradise of her childhood. She herself was aware that her writings had their origin in what she called her 'two kick offs'. In a letter to John Middleton Murry from Bandol in 1918 she wrote:

> Ive two 'kick offs' in the writing game. *One* is joy – real joy . . . The other 'kick off' is . . . an *extremely* deep sense of hopelessness – of everything doomed to disaster – almost wilfully, stupidly . . . *a cry against corruption.*

and she added:

> I am at present fully launched, right out in the deep sea with this second state...[1]

At the stime she was writing *'Je ne parle pas français'*. It is worth noting, too, that when she developed what J.M. Murry called 'the final phase'[2] in her writing she was to give vent to her joy in 'Prelude' and, shortly after, to her cry against corruption in *'Je ne parle pas français'*.

Before we proceed to examine some of her short stories, it may be in order to recall briefly what is meant by irony as a stylistic device or as narrative procedure. Irony has been defined as 'a figure of speech in which the idea intended to be conveyed is different from, usually the opposite of, the literal meaning of the words used'. As such it is close to sarcasm. In a broader sense it refers to 'a conflict between appearance and reality'. As such it is nearer to Socratic irony and implies disguise or deception, whether as flattery, condemnation, or reserve.³ Irony in a more complex sense again derives 'from a mode of perception that enables one to express an insight or attitude without sacrificing the complexities'.⁴ As a mode of perception irony often issues in a narrative procedure through which different, usually contradictory, views are held in balance so that each needs to be qualified through its relation to the other.

Let us now consider briefly two of Katherine Mansfield's early stories, both written in 1910 and first published in *In a German Pension* (1911).⁵

In 'Germans at Meat' the I-narrator, a young English woman, is a guest in a Bavarian pension and reports the German guests' conversation as well as her own reactions to it. The conversation starts off in what must have struck a young English, or New Zealand, girl of the early twentieth century as in bad taste: Herr Rat's remark that his *Magen* has not been in order for several days (p. 28). This leads on to talk about eating habits, particularly on English breakfasts. This talk on food, bodily functions, and ailments does not, however, put her off; any more than does the guests' criticism of English habits and mores. She manages to keep her good humour and to disguise what she is feeling. Only when the guests' aggressiveness towards England flares up and one of the guests assures her:

> We don't want England. If we did we would have had her long ago. We really do not want you. (p. 31)

is she driven to retort, a little pertly perhaps: 'We certainly do not want Germany' (p. 31).

The English girl's politeness is the more striking as the guests have revealed their aggressiveness and their sense of national superiority. It is, indeed, through their remarks that the German middle class of the Bismarckian era has been satirized: the women's absorption in the three K's — *Kirche, Küche, Kinder* — and the men's readiness to assert themselves militarily through another K, i.e. *Krieg*. Finally, the Widow, with unconscious humour, remarks:

> No wonder there is a repetition in England of that dreadful state of things in Paris . . . How can a woman expect to keep her husband if she does not know his favourite food after three years? (p. 31)

Although the *non sequitur* makes us laugh, the Widow's remark is an index to the German middle-class's sense of the sacred hierarchical order in society at the same time as it is a direct criticism of their guest. The narrator yet remains polite to the end, but she cannot bear any more of this: she wishes the German guests '*Mahlzeit!*' and leaves the room.

In this story the irony resides exclusively in the narrator's disguise or silencing of her feelings. True, the characters are caricatures, and the story is no more than a little satirical sketch. But Katherine Mansfield was quick to learn, as we see from the next story in that collection, 'The Baron'.

Here again Katherine Mansfield uses as a narrator a young English woman who witnesses the German guests' behaviour and discovers their opinions and prejudices. This time, however, the narrator's view of the Baron will need to be corrected; as a consequence, the picture sounds truer to life and less satirical.

The situation is again meals the guests of a pension take together, except for the Baron, who always sits alone with his back to the others, an exclusiveness which the German guests find quite appropriate since he is 'the First of the Barons' (p. 33) and as such far above the other guests. This attitude of theirs elicits the narrator's pity for the Baron, who seems to her to be debarred 'from the pleasures of intellectual intercourse' (p. 31). The vulgarity of these people is all the more striking as their names denote a higher social status, and all the more ridiculous since all their comments show that their only yardsticks are class and money.

More amusing is the twist given to the story by the narrator's discovery that the Baron *chooses* to eat alone, and why. One evening she is caught in the rain and, as she hesitates to cross the slushy road, the Baron asks her to share his umbrella. He then explains to her:

> I sit alone that I may eat more . . . my stomach requires a great deal of food. I order double portions, and eat them in peace. (p. 34)

On her return to the pension with the Baron she thanks him *audibly* from the landing, while he, the polite gentleman, shares unwittingly in the joke by replying equally loudly 'Not at all!', so that all the guests can hear him too. From then on the Germans will treat the narrator with respect, convinced as they are that she now has a proper regard for the Baron, and that he himself treats her with due courtesy.

The Baron leaves the next day, and the narrator concludes: 'Sic transit gloria German mundi', a remark which expresses a far more complex response to the situation as a whole than any we have been led to form as we progressed through the narrative.

Compared with 'Germans at Meat', this story shows a considerable advance in narrative technique. Not only is the narrator's pity for the Baron shown to have been without foundation, but he turns out to be simply a big eater and thus becomes a figure of fun: he is neither the poor fellow excluded from the community as the narrator thought, nor the awe-inspiring figure such as the Germans' snobbishness had made him out to be. The tables have thus been turned not only on the narrator and on the guests, but on the readers too, for we were first ready to share the narrator's pity for the Baron and her — implied — condemnation of the other guests' sense of class distinctions. In the end, then, it is all a matter for laughter since all have been mistaken in one way or another. The narrator's conclusion, 'Sic transit gloria German mundi' conveys the view of the detached observer, a view that includes her awareness of the German guests' disappointment at this inevitable return to their humdrum life, as well as her own sense of the vanity of their respect for status. It is almost as though she were saying — with the same tolerant good humour as Puck in *Midsummer Night's Dream* — 'What fools these mortals be'.

'Je ne parle pas français' (written in 1918, published in *Bliss and Other Stories,* 1920) is a subtler and more complex story, at once more radically critical and more poignant. Again, the story is told by an I-narrator, Raoul Duquette, whose self-portrait is, in fact, the centre of interest, but whose character cannot be assessed rightly unless one takes into account the ironical treatment of him by the author, that is, the discrepancy between his own view of himself and what he turns out to be.

Duquette presents himself at the beginning as a regular frequenter of a little café in Paris, where he can watch the habitués. His fascination with people, we gather, is that of a man who delights in catching them at their worst and savours his triumph. He next proceeds to evoke that experience.

Late on that first evening, when the café was quiet and the waiter was strewing straw over the floor, he felt that

> one would not have been surprised, if the door had opened and the Virgin Mary had come in, riding upon an ass, her meek hands folded over her big belly. (p. 279)

Whatever construction we put upon this image of innocent maternity in this context, we are struck by Duquette's self-satisfaction at this *trouvaille*, for, addressing the reader, he comments:

> That's rather nice, don't you think, that bit about the Virgin? It comes from the pen so gently; it has such a 'dying fall'. I thought so at the time and decided to make a note of it. One never knows when a little tag like that may come in useful to round off a paragraph. (p. 279)

This reaction betrays one aspect of him as a writer, i.e. the *aesthete*. Reaching for his writing-pad to jot down his *trouvaille*, he was brought up short on seeing on it 'that stupid, stale little phrase: *Je ne parle pas français*' (p. 280), and he was suddenly overwhelmed with a sense of agony. Although the significance of the French phrase will not appear until the end of the story, the intensity of the feeling Duquette experiences is rather surprising. Yet no sooner had he felt this keen sense of agony, he tells us, than he was already thinking, as he remembers:

> Good God! Am I capable of feeling as strongly as that? . . . After all I must be first-rate. No second-rate mind could have experienced such an intensity of feeling so . . . purely. (p. 280)

The sudden sense of agony, it thus appears, only served to confirm his pride in being a first-rate mind. Besides he has told us that the rule of his life is

> never to regret and never to look back. Regret is an appalling waste of energy, and no one who intends to be a writer can afford to indulge in it. . . . It's keeping yourself poor. Art can't and won't stand poverty. (p. 280)

In the next section Duquette presents himself as he now is, that is, as a true Parisian, a representative of a social and cultural group to which he is proud of belonging, one that we associate with the 'emancipated' writers Katherine Mansfield had encountered in the Paris of Francis Carco in 1913.[6] The more Duquette tells us about himself, the more odious he appears as a person and as a writer. He boasts of being rootless: he has no family and he does not want one; the only memory from his childhood that has survived is one that has taught him how to get people to do what he wants and has helped him to get on in the world. He even boasts of the ease with which, without his ever making the first advances to any woman, he always found some ready to see him through his money difficulties; in fact, he as good as tells us of his success as a gigolo. Moreover, we gather that he takes a meretricious view of his work as a writer. Yet he boasts of all this, that is, of his selfishness and of his perversion. By now we have realized, too, that the world in which Duquette postures as a serious artist, and of which we soon have a glimpse at the publisher's party, must have a strange sense of values, literary or other.[7]

Duquette then launches on the narrative of his relations with Dick Harmon, which falls into three parts: first, his meeting with him and the kind of relation that developed between them; second, the way they parted; and third, — much the longest part — his relation with Dick when the latter returned to Paris with a woman friend, and abruptly left her alone.

At his first meeting with Dick Duquette was prompted to tell him 'everything as sincerely and truthfully as [he] could', he says, taking

> immense pains to explain things about [his] submerged life that really were disgusting and never could possibly see the light of literary day. (p. 285)

And he adds that, in fact, he made himself out to be 'far worse than [he] was — more boastful, more cynical, more calculating'. From the way he relates their conversation it is clear that he emphasized this disgusting side of himself in order to impress Dick, who, however, merely commented: 'very curious' or 'very interesting', or 'very curious and interesting'. Obviously, he was making himself out to be the *mauvais garçon,* acting a part which no doubt suited him, but a part all the same. No wonder the photograph of Dick's mother that dropped out of his pocket-book should have seemed to be saying: 'Out of my sight, you little perfumed fox-terrier of a Frenchman' (p. 286).

Duquette and Dick parted abruptly one evening when Dick announced that he was leaving for England the next day. Duquette was naturally taken aback by this sudden decision, but more important, he felt *insulted* and nursed this sense of insult even after Dick had written him a friendly letter. Duquette's self-centredness appears again when, a few months later, as he relates, he received a letter from Dick, whom, by his own admission and in accordance with his rule of life, he had almost forgotten. Dick was writing that he was coming back to Paris, 'bringing a woman friend with him' (p. 287), and asked Duquette to take rooms for him. 'Of course I would', Duquette tells us, and continues:

> Away the little fox-terrier flew. *It happened most usefully, too; for I owed much money at the hotel where I took my meals, and two English people requiring rooms for an indefinite time was an excellent sum on account.* (p. 287, my italics)

The third part of Duquette's narrative deals first with his meeting with Dick and his woman friend at the station, when, on being introduced to Duquette, the young woman — whom Dick calls Mouse — apologizes, saying: *'Je ne parle pas français'*. Duquette next relates how he helped them, that is, pretending to act as the faithful friend and helpful host while not only making a good bargain for himself, but unable — or unwilling — to hide his coarseness from us.

Mouse, we have by now realized, is the person whom Duquette remembered nostalgically on finding on his writing-pad the 'stupid, stale little phrase' which triggered the narrative. By now, too, we know Duquette to be one of those people who regard themselves as superior to the general run of men and are ready to use others for their own purpose. The narrative ultimately shows him to be what *he* considers a devotee to art, in fact, what *we* feel to be a hollow man with his heart if not his head filled with straw. He is not only the poseur for ever thinking of the effect he is producing, he is also the voyeur, as appears after Dick's cowardly flight.

The last part of the story shows even more tellingly that Duquette has no respect for the heart's affections, that he is, in fact, nothing but an egoist and a sensation-monger. Most sickening of all is the callousness of his reaction to Dick's letter: far from being shocked by it as we all are, all he thought at the time was that it was 'a rare find': although Mouse was clearly at a loss, as if the bottom had fallen out of her world, Duquette experienced 'a wonderful sense of elation' as he felt:

> I was even — more than even with my 'that's very curious and interesting' Englishman. . . . (p. 297)

He was remembering Dick's failure to be impressed by Duquette's confession about his 'submerged life'. When confronted with Mouse, who had just admitted that 'there [was] something the matter' and had added:

> No, I'm afraid you can't help, thank you . . . I'm awfully sorry. It must be horrid for you. (p. 295)

Duquette thought, as he reports:

> Horrid, indeed! Ah, why couldn't I tell her that it was months and months since I had been so *entertained?* (p. 295, my italics)

It is almost as if he were boasting to us of his utter heartlessness. After relating that he left Mouse with a promise to return the next morning, he comments:

> Not until I was half-way down the boulevard did it come over me — the full force of it.
> Why, they were suffering . . . those two . . . really suffering. (p. 298)

And he adds that at the time he felt : 'I have seen two people suffer as I don't suppose I ever shall again' (p. 298); from which we infer that he intended to treasure that 'experience' as he had treasured the image of the Virgin, thus proving once again to be more concerned with what as a writer he regards as an addition to his stock of experiences than with the suffering of his friends. As it turns out, not even his curiosity could prompt him to try and help Mouse, so he never went to see her again.

Duquette, the cynic, appropriately concludes his narrative on a sentimental note. Mouse's last words, conveying her helplessness on being left alone in Paris, were once again: *'Je ne parle pas français'*; to Duquette, these words were, he says, 'her swan song' (p. 298). Although he exclaims towards the end: 'But how she makes me break my rule' (p. 299), obviously, his rule never to regret, he ends with an evocation of both his later dreams of Mouse and of his offer of a little girl to 'some dirty old gallant' who came up to his table in the little café. This last note aptly rounds off the portrait of the corrupt man and perverted writer.

The story does present a devastating picture of a Parisian writer. Virginia Woolf disliked it because, she said, it breathes nothing but hate. Yet the dominant note, I would argue, is one of horror, as though the author, awed by such evil, had exclaimed, like Conrad's Kurtz, 'the horror, the horror'. It *is* a picture of perversion, but I believe it was not written with a sting, as Katherine Mansfield feared her reader might feel,[8] but with a passionate sense that human and artistic values cannot be dissociated. It is, indeed, *a cry against corruption.*

Compared with Duquette's perversion, Dick's evasion of responsibilities, however unpalatable, is a minor shortcoming, one, however, which, underlining as it does man's responsibility for other men, is a variation on the main theme, both aspects of which betray the sense of hopelessness from which the story sprang. This impression is all the stronger because the pathetic figure of Mouse haunts us from early on in the story, even before we have grasped that it is her fate to be abandoned by the two men, a situation, indeed, which inevitably recalls that of Katherine Mansfield in 1913, when J.M. Murry left her in Paris to return to London. That, no doubt, was the germ of the story. However, the author has managed to transcend her personal experience by having the situation presented objectively, that is, through a narrator who throws into relief his own character.

For all this the author's sense of hopelessness comes through to us. Although Dick's flight from Paris and the explanation he leaves behind is the source of Mouse's intense suffering, this is muted in the story through the foregrounding of the portrait of the Parisian writer. Katherine Mansfield's personal sense of hopelessness is thereby extended into a cry against corruption, the corruption of such writers as Duquette and of those to whom he owes his success. Her development from the early caricature of 'Germans at Meat' to the comedy of 'The Baron' thus found its ultimate achievement in this radical criticism of the perverted artist, coupled as it is in *'Je ne parle pas français'* with the poignancy of the helpless Mouse, a victim of the distortion of human and aesthetic values.

NOTES

1. Letter to John Middleton Murry, 3 February 1918, in *Collected Letters of Katherine Mansfield*, edited by Vincent O'Sullivan with Margaret Scott, vol. 2 (Oxford: Clarendon Press, 1987), p. 54.

2. *The Short Stories of Katherine Mansfield*, edited by J.M. Murry (New York: Alfred Knopf, 1937), Introduction, p. vii.

3. *A Handbook of Literary Terms,* compiled by H.L. Yelland, S.C. Jones and K.S.W. Easton (Sydney and London: Angus and Robertson, 1950, 1953), p. 100.

4. *Poems for Study*, edited by Leonard Unger and William Van O'Connor (New York: Rinehart, 1953), Introduction, p. 17.

5. As A. Alpers remarks: 'The wave of anti-German feeling in England at the time [viz. 1911] had something to do with [the favourable reception of *In a German Pension*], but the book was well received', *Katherine Mansfield. A Biography* (London: Jonathan Cape, 1954, 1956), p. 144. Katherine Mansfield forbade the reprinting of this collection in 1914 and in 1920 (see Alpers, op. cit., pp. 204, 288) and again in 1922 (see Claire Tomalin, *Katherine Mansfield. A Secret Life* (London: Viking, 1987), p. 209). J.M. Murry first re-issued *In a German Pension* in 1927.

6. In a letter to J.M. Murry of 4 February 1918, a continuation of the letter quoted above (see note 1), Katherine Mansfield explains: 'The subject I mean lui qui parle is of course taken from — Carco & Gertler & God knows who. It has been more or less in my mind ever since I first felt strongly about the french', in *Collected Letters of Katherine Mansfield*, edited by Vincent O'Sullivan with Margaret Scott, vol. 2 (Oxford: Clarendon Press, 1987), p. 56.

7. Duquette himself at one point compares himself to 'a little woman in a café who has to introduce herself with a handful of photographs' (p. 283), thereby equating his writing with a loathsome trade.

8. In the letter of 4 February 1918, referred to in note 6, Katherine Mansfield continues: 'I hope youll see (of course you will) that I am not writing with a sting'.

Katherine Mansfield's 'Nouvelle-Instant'

RENÉ GODENNE

> ... une oeuvre d'art
> totale en elle-même...
> Marcel Brion

I have never read Katherine Mansfield's works in English[1] but, as a historian of the French short story, I have very often quoted her texts as necessary reference points for a whole generation of short-story writers in the French-speaking world.[2]

It is now well established that Katherine Mansfield's short stories offered a new concept of the genre to the French literary world of the early twentieth century: until then the art of the short story established by Maupassant and his successors, and before them by the romantic short story writers, had indeed been quite different.[3] For Katherine Mansfield, the short-story no longer told a 'story' in the traditional sense of the word. In 1928 Marcel Brion made this point in his review of 'Bliss': 'the aesthetics of the short story is exactly the opposite of that of the novel: to the linear development of the novel Katherine Mansfield opposes the presentation of a single moment. Instead of describing the existence of individuals in a series of events, she describes brief everyday dramas. By means of a "cross-section", a "swab", she introduces the reader to their private lives by presenting them during a particularly significant moment'.[4]

The celebration of the centenary of her birth therefore seems to be the right moment for me to study Katherine Mansfield's own conception of the short story.

Among the seventy-nine texts available in French, sixty-five can be called 'nouvelles-instants'[5] or, to use Marcel Brion's terms, 'prélèvements' or 'coupes' in the lives of a few individuals.

In these sixty-five stories, the action never occupies but a brief period of time. The titles themselves are sometimes explicit because they at once imply and circumscribe an exact duration of time: 'Frau Brechenmacher Attends a Wedding', 'A Birthday', 'Mr Reginald Peacock's Day', 'Bank Holiday'. In other stories the temporal limits of the subject can be precisely determined, for the author has used a variety of time markers throughout the texts (I have counted more than two hundred) that allow the reader to perceive the passage of time within a limited time-span. Katherine Mansfield organizes, controls, and structures any length of time perfectly. A time marker is often given right at the beginning of the story: 'Four of the clock one July afternoon . . .' ('Frau Fischer', p. 52). The author times the action as it unwinds: 'Every few minutes one of the children asked him the question' ('Prelude', p. 227); 'she took out her silver watch to look at the time. Half-past four' ('The Little Governess', p. 171). The passage of time can also be marked by other means, such as the following:

> Bread soup was placed upon the table . . . The servant brought in veal, with 'sauerkraut' and potatoes . . . The dishes were changed for beef, red currants and spinach . . . A glass dish of stewed apricots was placed upon the table . . . They were handed cherry cake with whipped cream. ('Germans at Meat', pp. 28-31)

The time pattern of 'The Garden Party' is typical in this respect:

> Breakfast was not yet over . . . And what a beautiful morning . . . Lunch was over by half-past one . . . And the perfect afternoon slowly ripened, slowly faded, slowly its petals closed. . . . It was just growing dusky. (pp. 487-497)

It is therefore not surprising that in most of the texts time can be determined quite accurately: one day (11 occurrences), an afternoon (8), a morning (6), an evening (6), from afternoon to evening (6). Occasionally, the time-span is very short: a few hours (5 occurrences: from 4 o'clock to 6:30 in 'Frau Fischer', from 8 o'clock to 13:30 in 'Revelations', etc.); one hour (2 occurrences: 'The Fly', for example).[6] Even when no indication of time is given, and such is the case in nine of the stories, it is clear that the time-span doesn't extend beyond a few hours. On the other hand, six stories, including 'Prelude', cover a considerably longer period of time: two days (2 occurrences), three days (2), one week (2): 'after the most awful week of my life' ('Prelude', p. 256). In such cases the chronological movement is not continuous, as was the case in the texts mentioned above: the narration jumps from one moment to another. The structure of 'Prelude' is a good example: the narrative is focused on twelve isolated moments presented in twelve separate sections within the course of one week. 'The Garden Party' follows the same pattern: twelve different moments experienced by different characters in one day.

Once the time is clearly established, the subject of the 'nouvelle-instant' is developed around a limited number of daily events that can be labelled as common or even banal: settling into a new house ('Prelude'), a meal ('Germans at Meat'), a journey, the most frequent situation ('The Journey to Bruges'), a walk ('The Escape'), a reception ('Sun and Moon'), a conversation ('Two Tuppenny Ones Please'), or simply the unfolding of a day ('Sixpence'). In each instance the unprepared reader enters *ex abrupto* into a particular situation about which he knows little or nothing about the characters *before* the chosen moment. This situation can be one of two types: the habitual (17 times) or the unique (46 times). In the habitual situation, the author simply chooses a moment from the lives of a few individuals — a moment typical of their lives past or to come ('The Wind Blows', 'The Man Without a Temperament', 'Marriage à la Mode'). In the unique situation the author catches hold of a never-to-be-repeated moment. As the following examples show, Katherine Mansfield resorts to identical words, as if only these were possible. A moment of intense happiness: 'For the first time in her life Bertha Young desired her husband' ('Bliss', p. 314), 'she realised that now at last for the first time in her life — she had never imagined any feeling like it before — she knew what it was to be in love, *but — in — love*!' ('Taking the Veil', p. 529). A moment of infinite distress: 'It was too much — she'd had too much in her life to bear' ('Life of Ma Parker', p. 407). A moment that might change one's life: 'He'd missed it. It was too late to do anything now. Was it too late? Yes, it was' ('Psychology', p. 322), 'Ah, God! What had she done! . . . Was it too late? Could it be too late?' ('A Dill Pickle', p. 276). The French translator of the story even uses the very term 'instant' and 'moment' for such phrases: 'As it was [à ce moment] she felt a rush of love for George' ('Honeymoon', p. 536), 'But when she answered I knew from her voice the moment [cet instant] was over for now [momentanément du moins]' ('Poison', p. 380).

Habitual or unique, the moment describes states of being which, if they are final, consist of *evocations* (34 times: e.g., 'Germans at Meat', 'The Wind Blows', 'Bank Holiday', 'Spring Pictures', 'At the Bay'). If these states are the consequence of new and unexpected situations experienced by the characters, they present a new awareness triggered off by a moment of *revelation*. It is noteworthy that the word appears 30 times and once in a title: 'That evening for the first time in his life, as he pressed through the swing door and descended the three broad steps to the pavement, old Mr Neave felt he was too old for the spring' ('An Ideal Family', p. 421). It is hard not to think of the exemplary story 'Bliss':[7] Bertha is receiving guests; she is happy, tremendously happy, until she notices her husband courting another woman. There are further examples of this: a young girl discovers social misery ('The Garden Party'); at the sight of her lover wearing a cap instead of his usual hat, a married woman decides not to run away with him ('The Black Cap').[8] In stories such as these, the subject is the appearance of a disruptive element, be it a character or a set of circumstances, that produces a dramatic break in the established order. Contrary to the 'nouvelle-évocation', the driving force of the 'nouvelle-révélation' is its drama, which confers a serious, even pathetic dimension on the subject. This dimension is even more apparent when the end of the story is left open (10 times): the situation remains suspended and therefore unresolved while the order has been permanently disrupted. The last lines of 'Bliss' are exemplary in this respect: ' "Oh, what is going to happen now?" she cried' (p. 315). Just as evocative are the last lines of 'The Stranger': 'Spoilt their evening! Spoilt their being alone together! They would never be alone together again' (p. 373), and this passage from 'Life of Ma Parker', this old woman whose past life is so sad and who is so tired of life:

> Oh, wasn't there anywhere where she could hide and keep herself to herself and stay as long as she liked, not disturbing anybody, and nobody worrying her? Wasn't there anywhere in the world where she could have her cry out — at last?
> Ma Parker stood, looking up and down. The icy wind blew out her apron into a balloon. And now it began to rain. There was nowhere. (p. 408)[9]

Unlike Marcel Arland or Stéphanie Corinna Bille, for example, Katherine Mansfield has a preference for closing the moment (54 times) that indicates a determination to remain within the same moment, which is presented in the last lines as a closed universe. Such closure, however, still manages to convey a tremendous evocative power, as evidenced by the ending of 'At the Bay':

> A cloud, small, serene, floated across the moon. In that moment of darkness the sea sounded deep, troubled. Then the cloud sailed away, and the sound of the sea was a vague murmur, as though it waked out of a dark dream. All was still. (p. 469)

Katherine Mansfield's 'nouvelle-instant' is defined by the absence of anecdote: she presents states of being, and all that counts for the reader is the exploration, psychological or other, of a situation and of its effects on the characters. All that matters is the substance of a moment. This is why the author frequently does not name the characters: 'the stranger', 'the young man', 'the friend', 'the boss'... This is also why she isolates in different texts moments lived in succession by the same characters: 'Epilogue I: Pension Seguin' and 'Epilogue II: Violet' ('after my first night at the *Pension Seguin*', p. 142), 'The Journey to Bruges' (i.e., on the way to the city) and 'Being a Truthful Adventure' (i.e., in the city). Ultimately this allows her to juxtapose evocations that have no apparent links between them — in 'See-Saw' and 'Spring Pictures'. At first glance, some titles appear to be those of 'real' stories; but a closer look reveals that this is not the case: 'How Pearl Button Was Kidnapped' deals with a little girl living happily among her gypsy captors, 'Being a Truthful Adventure' presents a walk in Bruges, 'A Suburban Fairy Tale' describes a family meal. Yet some stories take a different approach and the author may give more importance to the plot by focusing on a less banal and more peculiar subject: the day of a woman who helps a murderer ('Millie'); the day of a woman who must find a new job and cannot find one ('Pictures'); the day of a battered child who smothers the baby placed in her charge ('The Child-Who-Was-Tired'); a woman confesses to her husband that a man died in her arms ('The Stranger'). Each time, however, Katherine Mansfield cuts short the plot interest: the odd event often remains unexplained (the assassin's deed, the dead person) and is used only as an element of the story, not as the cause of the drama as it would in a plot story. It is significant that the battered child's deed occurs at the end of the story thereby leaving the story open as it were.

A special feature of Katherine Mansfield's technique is that sometimes she altogether eliminates the narrative from her texts.[10] This is achieved in two ways. The author takes a 'cross-section' of a particular situation and dwells only on its important atomic elements: in 'Mr Reginald Peacock's Day', for instance, the story's focus shifts without transition from the first 'moment' (presenting Reginald Peacock, a salon artist, dreaming about the spectacular evening to come only in order to forget about the house-wife who is his spouse) to the second (when one night, he comes home drunk and murmurs to his sleeping wife the name of another woman). The condensed form of 'Marriage à la Mode' also comes to mind:

> But after supper they were all so tired they could do nothing but yawn until it was late enough to go to bed. . . .
> It was not until William was waiting for his taxi the next afternoon that he found himself alone with Isabel. (p. 437)

Not only is the focus on a particular subject, but more typically, on what is essential to this subject.

The absence of 'plot' is more apparent in other texts. Either the short story becomes a type of playlet, as in 'Two Tuppenny Ones Please', or the narration is replaced by parenthetical stage directions as, for instance, in the introduction of 'Late at Night': '(*Virginia is seated by the fire. Her outdoor things are thrown on a chair; her boots are faintly steaming in the fender.*)' (p. 205); or '(The real Rosabel, the girl crouched on the floor in the dark, laughed aloud, and put her hand up to her hot mouth.)' ('The Tiredness of Rosabel', p. 20). This is the type of phrase that punctuates the progression of the narrative. The most telling example of this procedure is no doubt the way in which narrative development is indicated in 'The Black Cap'; every privileged moment is announced by means of parenthetical stage directions:

> (*A lady and her husband are seated at breakfast. He is quite calm, reading the newspaper and eating; but she is strangely excited, dressed for travelling, and only pretending to eat.*) (p. 207)

Other stage directions mark the development of the action: on the way to the station, at the station, arrival of the characters, etc.

As previously noted, among the 79 stories presented in the French editions of Katherine Mansfield's fiction, 65 are 'nouvelles-instants'; Katherine Mansfield's conception of the short story could not be more clear. However, in 14 instances, she tells 'stories': a man sees one of his friends refuse to live with a woman in order to remain with his mother ('*Je ne parle pas français*'); alone in Paris, a young painter falls in love with a woman whom he does not dare to approach ('Feuille d'Album'); young girls from a bourgeois family invite their classmates to admire their new doll's house and when the turn of the two children of a laundry-woman comes, they are chased away ('The Doll's House'). Yet, even in such stories it is only on the surface that Katherine Mansfield is a 'story' teller: the notion of 'instant', as she sees it, remains omnipresent. '*Je ne parle pas français*' is 'enclosed' within two 'instants': in a café a man reminisces; freed from the weight of the past, he leaves the café. The reflections of the protagonists in 'The Lady's Maid' and in 'Bad Idea' fit within the framework of an 'instant'. 'Widowed' consists of two distinct moments: the morning of a happy woman with a man; the dramatic day when her husband died. 'The Canary', 'A Married Man's Story', and 'Something Childish But Very Natural' present a succession of isolated moments. The structure of the latter story is exemplary: 1. a Friday, 2. a Monday, 3. the passage of a week's time based only on the contents of two letters, 4. a Saturday, 5. an evening, 6. a day, 7. a day. Each of them could actually be read as a 'nouvelle-instant'. It is no accident that the term 'instant' appears in the French translation of '*Je ne parle pas français*' for the phrase: 'I enjoyed one of these moments the first time I ever came in here' (p. 278). Further evidence can be found in the open and very strong ending of 'Something Childish But Very Natural', in which we see a man realizing that the woman he loves will not come to meet him:

> The garden became full of shadows — they span a web of darkness over the cottage and the trees and Henry and the telegram. But Henry did not move. (p. 166)

The only criterion that in the end distinguishes the two types of story is that of duration: on the one hand a clear pause in time, on the other an overview of a less precise duration of time; this is one more way of showing that for Katherine Mansfield the keystone of the short story is really the moment. Moreover, even her apparently more classical stories are not based on plot, as would normally be expected from that kind of story: 'Feuille d'Album' ends at the moment when a love affair begins; in 'A Bad Idea', an allusion is made to a 'catastrophe' but the reader will never know which one. The following sentences from 'A Married Man's Story' — which have so often been quoted — beautifully summarize the intention: 'That is how I long to write. No fine effects — no bravuras. But just the plain truth, as only a liar can tell it' (p. 481).

To define more fully the art and the talent of Katherine Mansfield as a short-story writer would also involve the analysis of other aspects of her technique: the art of being brief, of endowing the most banal and most common with the greatest human dimension, of suggesting rather than describing (a great depth of observation, combined with a keen sense of the meaningful detail), the natural ease of the dialogues, the power of phrases such as

> His heart fell out of the side window of his studio, and down to the balcony of the house opposite — buried itself in the pot of daffodils under the half-opened buds and spears of green ('Feuille d'Album', p. 269)

or

> He walked about with a shining ring of Edna keeping the world away or touching whatever it lighted on with its own beauty ('Something Childish But Very Natural', p. 162).

What should be conveyed is the very subtle and lasting *pleasure* of reading these texts whose appeal has not faded with time. What the French 'nouvelliste' Annie Saumont writes about her own short stories applies to Katherine Mansfield and could be viewed as a tribute to the pioneer of the modern short story:

> The realm of the short story is the moment. The moment as it was lived; the story opens, unfolds itself, and by doing so reveals and intensifies the moment, like a slow-motion picture. It is well-known that the experience of a moment contains the infinite. It is this infinity that must be set free. The short story is a spectography of the moment. There remains, of course, the anecdote, the events and their succession; but this is only the surface. All this diversity is gathered and condensed in the qualitative unity of the 'instant'. And that which moves the reader — the only thing he will remember — is the unique flavour of a unique moment. [11]

NOTES

1. This paper, read in French at the centenary conference in Liège, has been translated into English by Patricia Phillips.

2. Marcel Arland and Annie Saumon (both French), Marianne Pierson–Pierard (Belgian) and Stephanie Corinna Bille (Swiss). See also Marcelle Castelier who dedicated her *Aiguillages* (Neuchâtel: La Bâconnière, 1943) to the memory of Virginia Woolf and 'Kathleen Mansfield', and Paule Saint–Onge who mentions Katherine Mansfield in one of her stories (in *La Maîtresse, nouvelles* (Montréal: CLF, 1963) : 'One day, however, she found a strange comfort in one of Katherine Mansfield's characters because she too was afraid of new maternities. Her name was Linda and, as she was, like her, resting peacefully in her garden, she said to her baby playing in the sun: "I don't like babies".'(pp. 53–54). One should also mention the 'Prix Katherine Mansfield, ou Prix Littéraire de la Nouvelle Brève' created in Menton in 1960.

3. See René Godenne, *La nouvelle française* (Paris: Presses Universitaires de France, 1974), pp. 50–108.

4. He wrote in *Revue Hebdomadaire*, May 1928, p. 477: 'Katherine Mansfield a décrit quelques–uns de ces petits drames brefs qui constituent essentiellement le domaine de la nouvelle. L'esthétique de la *short story* est exactement contraire à celle du roman. Elle oppose à sa continuité le choix d'un seul moment; elle ne décrit pas l'existence d'êtres, mais au moyen d'une "coupe", d'un "prélèvement", elle nous initie à leurs existences intimes, elle nous les montre non dans un enchaînement de faits; mais dans un instant caractéristique.'

5. For the French translation of Katherine Mansfield's short stories see *Oeuvres romanesques* (Paris: Stock, 1966) and *Le voyage indiscret* (Paris: Seuil, 1950). For the critical history of the publication of the translations, see B.J. Kirkpatrick, *A Bibliography of Katherine Mansfield* (Oxford: Clarendon Press, forthcoming). The distribution of the 'nouvelles–instants' in the various collections is as follows: 9 out of 13 in *In a German Pension*, 12 out of 14 in *Bliss*, 14 out of 15 in *The Garden Party*, 5 out of 10 in *The Dove's Nest*, 8 out of 10 in *Something Childish* and all the 17 translated texts in *Le voyage indiscret*.

6. To be complete one should also add: from one day to the next night (2), from one night to the next day (1), from one day to the next day (1), from one evening to the next day (1).

7. Michel Dupuis and Pierre Maury were right to include 'Bliss' in their anthology *Les 20 meilleures nouvelles de la littérature mondiale* (Paris: Marabout, 1987).

8. See also 'The Little Governess', 'Frau Brechenmacher Attends a Wedding', 'The Child–Who–Was–Tired', 'Revelations', 'Miss Brill', 'Her First Ball', 'The Stranger', 'An Ideal Family', 'A Cup of Tea', 'How Pearl Button Was Kidnapped', 'Sixpence'.

9. See also 'The Little Governess', 'Miss Brill', 'Mr Reginald Peacock's Day', 'The Child–Who–Was–Tired'.

10. 54 texts are told in the third person, with occasional extensions of perspective which include reader, author and narrator: e.g., 'All the same, *we* cling to *our* last pleasures as the tree clings to its last leaves' ('The Fly', p. 529, italics mine).

11. Unpublished letter dated 26 February 1980.

'Is the master out or in?' or Katherine Mansfield's Twofold Vision of Self.

ANDRÉE-MARIE HARMAT

In a paper delivered in March 1988 in Nice for the European Association of Commonwealth Literature,[1] I attempted to tackle an aspect of what seems to me one of the most fundamental tenets of Katherine Mansfield's art: her polyphonic treatment of narrative matter and the particular procedures she uses in order to break the linearity of language and its basic incapacity to convey two meanings at a time. These procedures — as I tried to show — were derived for the most part from her professional familiarity with music. In what I intended as a first step in a more extensive analysis, I limited my study to the purely stylistic aspect of her writing, dealing only with the 'sound-sense' of her prose exemplified by sound-patterns and rhythmical motifs. In this paper I would like to explore another aspect of her polyphonic art and attempt to show how, through the particular use of symbolic images and specific narrative methods, she creates in the reader an impression of the simultaneous and parallel unfolding of several — and often contrary — meanings and of the manifold strands that constitute the human psyche.

Starting from the very striking mirror image, we will proceed to an enumeration of other polyphonic devices used for the same effect, and then conclude with an analysis of one of Katherine Mansfield's most patently contrapuntal stories whose very eloquent title leaves us in no doubt about the nature of its author's aims: 'Psychology'.

***

The image of the mirror ranks among Katherine Mansfield's most obsessive means of psychological revelation. In nearly all her best stories, a focal character involuntarily or deliberately encounters her or his own reflected image: Linda in 'Prelude', soon followed by Beryl in the same story; Bertha in 'Bliss'; Matilda in 'The Wind Blows'; Monica Tyrell in 'Revelations'; Laura in 'The Garden Party'; Raoul Duquette in *'Je ne parle pas français'*. And there are other obvious instances in less well-known stories.

The mirror, it is true, has been used for centuries as a means of introspective investigation; it appears in the oldest popular tales — we all remember the wicked queen in 'Snow-White', searching the mirror for a consoling image of her insuperable beauty. Romanticists also made use of it;[2] and we cannot help calling to mind Mallarmé's 'Hérodiade' :

> O miroir!
> Eau froide par l'ennui dans ton cadre gelée
> Que de fois et pendant des heures, désolée
> Des songes et cherchant mes souvenirs qui sont
> Comme des feuilles sous ta glace au trou profond,
> Je m'apparus en toi comme une ombre lointaine,
> Mais, horreur! des soirs, dans ta sévère fontaine,
> J'ai de mon rêve épars connu la nudité!

Note, incidentally, that Katherine Mansfield's affinities with German Romanticism and French Symbolism are in no way confined to this, as a study of her garden symbolism, for instance, might reveal.

The mirror is a privileged image inherited from the remotest beginnings of literary evocation: a privilege obviously due to its specific power of duplicating the corporeal appearance of human beings.

In Katherine Mansfield's stories, the mirror mainly connotes two antithetic human attitudes: repulsion or attraction. The feeling of repulsion experienced by some characters who look away whenever they pass mirrors is clearly symbolic of their desire to ignore the obscure motivations of their subliminal selves. This instinctive terror of self-knowledge may be, like Linda Burnell's in 'Prelude', the spontaneous recoiling from letting her deeper self be exposed to the captious look of the hostile objects around her. Obscurely sensing the latent life throbbing in the never really inanimate furniture of her bedroom, the supersensitive heroine feels that

> [The objects] were not deceived. THEY knew how frightened she was; THEY saw how she turned her head away as she passed the mirror. (p. 235)

For Matilda, in 'The Wind Blows', the crucial crisis — the 'wind' of the title — that blows her on from childhood into adolescence makes self-knowledge appalling; this is clearly revealed when

> she begins to plait her hair with shaking fingers, not daring to look in the glass. (p. 191)

Similarly, Monica Tyrell, standing at the decisive juncture between youthful frigidity and mature sensuality, first evades her reflected image: 'She didn't want to look at herself' ('Revelations', p. 344), just before the epiphanic climax of the story.

In 'The Garden Party', the focal character, Laura Sheridan, also shrinks from the humiliating discovery of her momentarily triumphant vanity; her reluctance to look at herself in the mirror symbolizes her desire to ignore the truth. Her mother holds up a hand-mirror before her eyes, but she significantly refuses to discover its merciless message: 'She couldn't look at herself; she turned aside' (p. 495).

Bertha's deportment at the beginning of 'Bliss' is more ambiguous; although experiencing the same kind of misgivings as Laura or Matilda, she nevertheless looks at herself:

> She hardly dared to look into the cold mirror — but she did look, and it gave her back a woman, radiant, with smiling, trembling lips, with big, dark eyes and an air of listening, waiting for something . . . divine to happen . . . that she knew must happen . . . infallibly. (p. 305)

Bertha is just hovering on the brink of self-discovery, and although incapable, as yet, of taking in the luminous countenance of the strange woman watching her from the depths of the mirror, she wavers between repulsion and attraction and thus stands half-way between the two human attitudes symbolically connoted by the mirror. It is precisely this unknown presence in the looking-glass that other characters want to encounter. For them, the test of the mirror amounts to a real splitting of the self. In 'Prelude', Beryl is irresistibly drawn to her youthful good-looking image, but what she discovers is 'a slim girl in white' (p. 257) who seems to exist separately and brings to her mind a puzzled interrogation. She wonders 'what . . . that creature in the glass [had] to do with her, and why . . . she [was] staring?'(p. 258). At such moments, a kind of mute dialogue may arise between the reflected image and the watching character: in *'Je ne parle pas français'*, Raoul Duquette addresses the 'radiant vision' (p. 282) in the mirror; in 'Pictures', Miss Moss admonishes 'the person in the glass' for looking desperate:

> But the person in the glass made an ugly face at her.
> 'You silly thing,' scolded Miss Moss. (p. 325)

As for 'the little governess', terrified of having to manage an incensed porter demanding more than his due for carrying her dress-basket, she finds courage in comforting the mirror face:

> 'But it's all over now,' she said . . . feeling in some way that it was more frightened than she. (p. 168)

Whether repelled or attracted by mirrors, Katherine Mansfield's characters are always presented as the sum of two independent selves. Their synchronous existence is clarified through the split evocation permitted by the looking-glass — a twofold image enabling the writer to convey the impression of simultaneous permanence and the 'harmonic' effect resulting from it. The mirror thus clearly appears as a revealer of the counterpoint of a conscious and a subconscious psychological life in each individual. A purely psychological revealer, therefore, different in its finality — but not in its capacity to create the illusion of simultaneity — from such images as the aloe in 'Prelude' or the pear-tree in 'Bliss'.[3]

***

The autonomous, deeper ego, however, may assume other forms than the reflected image: for many, it is just 'the other self', leading an uncontrollable life of its own in the most mysterious regions of the psyche. Raoul Duquette in *'Je ne parle pas français'* remarks to himself:

> All the while I wrote that last page my other self has been chasing up and down out in the dark there.(p. 280)

And further on in the same story he observes:

> I confess that something did whisper as, smiling, I put up the notebook: 'You — literary?' . . . But I didn't listen. (p. 288)

This attitude is reminiscent of Laura Sheridan's or Monica Tyrell's, shrinking from the merciless image which the mirror returns to them. For Beryl, confidently dreaming of devoted lovers in 'At the Bay', appalling doubts suddenly emerge from subconscious depths:

> 'But how do you know he is coming at all?' mocked a small voice within her.
> But Beryl dismissed it. She couldn't be left. Other people, perhaps, but not she. (p. 468)

And when a male figure appears in the dark and invites her to take a walk with him, the counterpoint of conscious and obscure impulses gives signs of its antagonistic persistence in her:

> Beryl shook her head. But already something stirred in her, something reared its head.
> The voice said, 'Frightened?' It mocked, 'Poor little girl!,
> 'Not in the least,' said she. As she spoke that weak thing within her seemed to uncoil, to grow suddenly tremendously strong; she longed to go! (p. 469)

This is nothing exceptional: all focal characters are thus endowed with a lurking mysterious self behind their visible one. In 'A Dill Pickle', it is 'that old self' (p. 276), sporadically surfacing, always at the wrong moment; in 'Six Years After', the 'beings' (p. 506) of two elderly married people are taken up in a surreptitious exchange while their unwitting owners are mutely sitting side by side; in 'A Married Man's Story', we are told about 'the owner, the second self inhabiting [human beings]' (p. 479). In all cases, it is always the fundamental dichotomy of the human psyche that is given polyphonic expression.

***

One of the most remarkable examples of the contrapuntal treatment of separate levels of consciousness in human beings is the story significantly — and we might say, ironically — entitled 'Psychology'. The two characters — a male novelist and a female playwright — are seen congenially talking shop over a cup of tea. As expert psychologists, they confidently launch into self-analysis, priding themselves upon their superior enjoyment of an unsentimental relationship. But the harmonics involuntarily awakened by their perfectly conscious 'performance' completely contravene their belief in a dispassionate friendship. As their subconscious sentimental involvement becomes more and more obtrusive and makes it clear to them that they have been thoroughly mistaken about themselves, they desperately try to take refuge in gestures and words belying the appalling revelation. The point lies in the fact that they are entirely mistaken about themselves: hence the counterpoint of outspoken words and gestures, conscious thoughts, and subconscious intimations, taking place simultaneously in the two characters.

All the narrative procedures used by Katherine Mansfield in this story concur to the same effect: to produce in the reader the impression of synchronousness. Such is her aim in the structure of the story, whose introductory phase, development and epilogue systematically unfold on two different levels, carefully arranged in order to create the illusion of simultaneity. The introductory stage is, in this respect, exemplary. Its two 'linear' parts, each corresponding to a different level of consciousness, are so perfectly symmetrical that the first thirteen lines seem to be still ringing in our ears while we read their signifyingly modified repetition in the next ten. Katherine Mansfield's achievement — to bring out meaningful vibrations from the illusive simultaneity of voices that might be written on two parallel staves — is particularly convincing in the analogous dialogues at the core of each part. One is an outspoken exchange between the two characters, the other is supposed to be 'whispered' by 'their secret selves'; the total effect aimed at is schematized in the following graphic reproduction of Katherine Mansfield's polyphonic purpose:

1 – outspoken words: 'Not busy?' 'No, just going to have tea.'
2 – mute exchange: 'Why should we speak? Isn't this enough?'

1 – 'And you are not expecting anybody?' 'Nobody at all.'
2 – 'More than enough. I never realized until this moment. . . .'

1 – 'Ah! That's good.'
2 – 'How good it is just to be with you. . . .' 'Like this. . . .'

1 – . . . .
2 – 'It's more than enough.' (p. 318)

The unfinished sentences in the lower voice, indiscriminatingly emanating from one or the other of the two partners, very aptly suggest that, at this deep half-unconscious level, their perfect agreement is voiced in unison.

Katherine Mansfield systematically juxtaposes spoken dialogues and their mute counterparts in the subsequent development of the story — a story that might be entirely transcribed on two staves. The multi-dimensionality of narrative matter is indeed fundamental here and takes the place of a plot,[4] with all the customary requisites. The exposition presents the conflicting conscious and subconscious voices of the counterpoint. The dynamic development that follows can be divided into several stages. In the first (from p. 318, l. 23 to p. 320, l. 11) the characters' erroneous self-analysis is entirely vented through spoken words and conscious interior monologues; a second and a third moments (from p. 320, l. 11 to l. 39 and from p. 320, l. 40 to p. 321, l. 29 respectively) follow the ascending curve of the ambiguous conflict between conscious motivations and more and more compelling inarticulate impulses, and lead to a climactic scene (from p. 321, l. 30 to p. 322, l. 27) in which the continual presence of the deeper subconscious voice of the psychological counterpoint seems to assert its triumph. The final sequence of this climactic stage calls to mind the 'stretto' closing a fugue, in which all the contrasting voices seem to fuse so closely that the resulting harmony sounds indissoluble. The abrupt anti-climax in which gestures and words vigorously contradict the characters' epiphany would lead to the triumph of consciousness[5] were it not for the unexpected dénouement in the epilogue (from p. 322, l. 28 to the end). An abridged modified repetition of the story's situation[6] enables the female character to reconcile her conscious and subconscious inclinations while the open ending allows us to foresee the two partners' surrender to their genuine deeper feelings.

Synchronous effects do not appear only in the structure of the narrative. The same word may operate on two different levels and thus acquire a signifying verticality. The noun 'silence', for instance, is clearly ambivalent; it may be associated with the evocation of fallacious feelings occurring in the characters' clear consciousness:

> That silence could be contained in the circle of warm, delightful fire and lamplight. (p. 320)

But it can also connote the emergence of subconscious emotions and is then described as 'a new silence' (p. 320) which can be mentioned again in the climactic stage without any explanatory adjective:

> And now the silence put a spell upon them like solemn music. (p. 321)

The symbolic system of the story is also carefully contrived to underline the contrapuntal organization of the narrative. Thus, 'the circle of fire and lamplight', which is evocative of a magic circle imprisoning the two characters and standing for the trap of their fallacious relationship, is significantly used as the appropriate setting for their conscious exchanges. Its systematic counterpart, intimating the momentary triumph of their 'secret selves', is the pool of darkness whose 'ripples' flow 'away, away — boundlessly far — into deep glittering darkness' (p. 320). The notions of mystery, remoteness and darkness associated with it are regularly contrasted with those of fire, light and circular configuration: hence the metaphorical evocation of the characters,

> conscious of the boundless, questioning dark . . . . two hunters, bending over their fire, but hearing suddenly from the jungle beyond a shake of wind and a loud, questioning cry. . . . (p. 321)

A similar contrapuntal effect is achieved through the systematic alternation at ever decreasing intervals (all along the already mentioned ascending movement of the narrative) of motion and motionlessness, speech and silence.

***

An exhaustive survey of polyphonic procedures in 'Psychology' would reach beyond the limits of this paper — and the story is no exception among Katherine Mansfield's finished works. The fact that she ironically considered herself as one of 'the young writers of today – trying simply to jump the psycho-analyst's claim' ('Psychology', p. 321), explains away her possibly excessive recourse to a systematization of harmonic implication. In other works, a subtler use of similar methods enables her to unveil not only the subconscious thoughts recurrently surfacing in her characters' psyches, but also more transcendental intimations. And we can conjecture from what might have been one of her best tales — the never completed 'A Married Man's Story' — to what pitch of perfection she might have brought her contrapuntal skill. As her slightly disenchanted hero ponders:

> how extraordinarily *shell-like* we are as we are — little creatures, peering out of the sentry-box at the gate . . . wan little servants, who never can say for certain, even, if the master is out or in. . . . (p. 480)

It is his creator's voice that we can hear, venting her acute sense of the elusiveness of 'the master', that is to say the deeper, submerged self, invisibly ruling over its helpless 'servant', the conscious superficial self. Evading the rigid chronological linearity of language, Katherine Mansfield has undeniably succeeded in making 'the master's' voice vibrate through that of 'the servant' which is often deceptive. She has rendered her stories strikingly comparable with those polyphonic scores composed for a single-voiced instrument in which contrapuntal effects are left to the interpreter, who recognizes among the linear unfolding of written notes those that belong to each voice and consequently highlights and differentiates them.

In this respect — more than in any other — Katherine Mansfield can be considered as a pioneer. And although she is not often considered a major figure in the history of English literature, we cannot but feel that she paved the way to such successful literary experiments as Aldous Huxley's very significantly entitled novel, *Point Counter Point*, in which musical procedures were imitated in order to organize the contrapuntal development of the characters' destinies.

NOTES

1. A.-M. Harmat, 'The "sound-sense" of Katherine Mansfield's Stories', paper delivered at the EACLALS Conference in Nice, 22-25 March 1988.

2. See Novalis, *Die Lehrlinge zu Sais*.

3. Both images have a transcendental rather than psychological purport.

4. Indeed, as the title clearly indicates, the true protagonists of this story are the different levels of consciousness and not the characters themselves.

5. Since the two characters separate without unveiling their secret emotions to each other.

6. The male partner is replaced by an old friend.

Katherine Mansfield, British or New Zealander — The Influence of Setting on Narrative Structure and Theme.

ANNE HOLDEN RØNNING

The problem of whether there is a link between setting in a narrative text and the author's background and origin is a complex one, particularly so in the case of Commonwealth writers. In some authors, such as Conrad, the influence of the early years gives to their work a kind of internationalism. Katherine Mansfield's picture of her childhood country is of a New Zealand where people live as they assume people do in the 'Old Country'. Their models are in fact non-contemporary and somewhat idealized. To my mind it is this which gives a special kind of atmosphere — a kind of international colonialism, if we can use such a word — to her work, and to that of some other Commonwealth writers.

The function of setting in a work of art is twofold: to place the story in time and place, and to provide elements which will create or contribute to the atmosphere of the story. In her New Zealand stories Katherine Mansfield seems to use setting in both its functions, whereas in most of her British, or European stories, as I would prefer to call them, the prime function of setting is to create atmosphere, which may of course vary from story to story. For example, 'Life of Ma Parker' is about a charwoman who, on the death of her grandson, loses all sense of purpose in life, and her attempts to cope with this new situation, only to find she has nowhere to go. Similarly, in 'The Man Without a Temperament', the reader is left with a feeling of a hopeless situation. The former is placed in London, the latter in Southern France, but the only features which enable us to place them geographically are the descriptions of the environment. Both these stories make use of flashbacks to create this atmosphere of hopelessness. In the New Zealand stories, on the other hand, in addition to a vivid depiction of natural phenomena in the setting, there is also a definite plot or theme.

The history of the reception of Katherine Mansfield's stories clearly shows that many critics thought she was not a New Zealander in her art.[1] Such an opinion indicates that the criterion is far from being coherently defined. Yet if we read the New Zealand stories edited by I. Gordon as a piece of continuous prose, we realize that a definite distinction should be made between her New Zealand and her European stories.

The stories about her native country constitute about half of her written production, and many of them call to mind a parallel to James Joyce's use of his native city in *Dubliners*. If the volume *Undiscovered Country* is read as a kind of novel, a specific atmosphere clearly emerges — for example, that of illusion and reality as seen in the fantasy world of the child, Kezia, and of the adult, Linda. Like Joyce, Katherine Mansfield draws on her own experience, and then generalizes it to portray family life in New Zealand. The setting for these stories is centred around her childhood home, their three houses together with the summer cottages at Day's Bay and Muritai. The conditions of life, particularly of the young girls, are strikingly 'Victorian' when compared with contemporary England.

In the three long stories, 'Prelude', 'At the Bay' and 'The Garden Party', the setting not only provides the outer framework for the action, but is an integral part of it: for example, 'Prelude' deals with the removal of the family to another house and with certain events during the first few days there. Even in 'The Little Girl', 'Her First Ball' and the various 'voyage' stories, in which the setting is less specifically stated, events and/or atmosphere leave no doubt as to where they take place.

In contrast the European stories are seldom placed geographically; even such stories as *'Je ne parle pas français'* and 'The Man Without a Temperament', where details and atmosphere are so obviously French, have a universal quality. 'Psychology' and 'Marriage à la Mode' could be satires of personal relationships anywhere, the latter set in any of the numerous house parties Katherine Mansfield went to. These plotless stories are 'happenings'.

The reasons for this difference in approach can probably be explained autobiographically by her break with her non-intellectual family, and with conventional New Zealand society which she characterizes as 'firmly held with the self-fashioned chains of slavery' with its' hopelessly insipid doctrine that love is the only thing in the world, taught, hammered into women, from generation to generation'[2]. This belief, together with problems attached to gaining her independence and freedom, made her at first despise everything associated with her New Zealand life. In London she took up the opportunities she had let slip when she spent three to four years at Queen's College, a period about which she wrote:

> my *wasted, wasted* early girlhood. My college life . . . might never have contained a book or a lecture. . . . I gathered and gathered and hid away, for that long 'winter' when I should re-discover all this treasure.[3]

Katherine Mansfield thus turned to personal problems as the major source material for her work. The strong feminist trait in her work stems no doubt from her own beliefs and experiences but also from her association with Orage and Beatrice Hastings at *The New Age*. However, to her the function of the artist was not to grind an axe, but to 'attempt to create his own world *in* this world'.[4]

At the same time, 1911-1913, the task of creating her own world in Britain did not prevent her writing three or four stories based on a trip into the volcanic region of the North Island. In those stories she attempts to portray a New Zealand which did not belong to the upper-middle class, those who had 'made it' and were financially and socially secure. In 'The Woman at the Store', 'Ole Underwood' and 'Millie' she relates character to environment in a land which was still culturally dependent on Britain. She brings out the emotional problems of living in the backwoods, the sense of isolation (neither Ole nor Millie have any one to talk to), and its effect on the individual. The parched landscapes emphasize, and may be symbolic of, the problematic situation of the character, and correlatively appeal to the reader's sympathy.

This warm understanding is lacking in *In a German Pension*, which dates from the same period. In these stories we are left with the impression that the author is not only satirizing the German way of life, but that she found it repulsive. She does not make fun of her New Zealand characters in the same way as she does of the Germans and, at times, of the British.

As is well known it was only after meeting her brother in London that she consciously turned to New Zealand themes. The often quoted *Journal* entry of 1916, after the death of Leslie, summarizes her new attitude:

> I feel no longer concerned with the same appearance of things. The people who lived or whom I wished to bring into my stories don't interest me any more. The plots of my stories leave me perfectly cold. . . . Now — now [I] want to write recollections of my own country. Yes, I want to write about my own country till I simply exhaust my store. . . . I want for one moment to make our undiscovered country leap into the eyes of the Old World. It must be mysterious, as though floating. It must take the breath. . . . all must be told with a sense of mystery, a radiance, an afterglow.[5]

And later, in 1917, in a letter to Dorothy Brett, she writes:

> You know, if the truth were known I have a perfect passion for the island where I was born. . . . And just as on those mornings white milky mists rise and uncover some beauty, then smother it again and then again disclose it. I tried to lift that mist from my people and let them be seen and then to hide them again. . .[6]

Katherine Mansfield not only states her avowed intention to write about New Zealand, but also defines neatly one of the narrative techniques she uses in much of her work, both New Zealand and European, possibly influenced by Post-Impressionism, i.e., that of the vignette or picture. In some stories such as 'Bank Holiday' we might well be looking at a painting as it is being described. This story opens as follows:

> A stout man with a pink face wears dingy white flannel trousers, a blue coat with a pink handkerchief showing, and a straw hat much too small for him, perched at the back of his head. (p. 350)

In the New Zealand stories it seems as if we are at the theatre; the curtain goes up and we see a stage set with characters who speak and act. This impression is confirmed by the division of the stories into 'scenes', especially in 'Prelude', 'The Garden Party', 'At the Bay' and 'A Married Man's Story'. The various scenes depict different aspects of the same family in circumstances occurring within a limited time-span, or at various stages of the characters' life. There is a random association of ideas from one scene to the next, but setting provides the unity of impression which Katherine Mansfield considered essential. A non-New Zealand story using this technique is 'The Daughters of the Late Colonel'. The setting provides a framework for the exploration of the outer and inner consciousness of the characters.

In the European stories two of the dominant narrative techniques are the interior monologue — as in 'Miss Brill' and 'The Lady's Maid', where the whole story is a well-sustained monologue — and the use of 'epiphany' in a manner similar to Joyce's. In the New Zealand stories, however, interior monologue, though used to portray the inner consciousness of the characters, mainly female ones, is only one aspect of the narrative technique.

The role of the narrator is also different. Many European stories are told by a first-person narrator, frequently a woman, who discusses personal problems, feelings and experiences. Sometimes the third-person narrator is used, but it is only in the New Zealand stories that Katherine Mansfield uses a child narrator (according to M.C. Bradbrook an expression of a young country)..[7] These stories are thus written as if based on experience remembered, providing a feeling of security, a sense of belonging, while the distance in time suggests objectivity in the approach. 'Objectivity' means here standing outside the events related: the narrator re-creates and re-experiences them from afar. I would like to suggest that it is the use of a child narrator that gives verisimilitude to the New Zealand stories, compared with the European ones and their self-centred characters.

The use of the child narrator gives a kind of Wordsworthian quality to Katherine Mansfield's narrative, a kind of 'recollection in tranquillity', and, as I see it, this is emphasized by the use of poetic symbols such as the aloe tree. The sun is a dominant feature of the New Zealand stories, and is expressive not so much of masculinity as of happiness: the weather is almost always fine, everything sparkles and gleams, and has the sense of mystery, radiance and afterglow she wrote about. Even the moon is usually portrayed as clear and shining, and with its silvery light it is here, as elsewhere in Katherine Mansfield, symbolic of the female. In 'The Wind Blows', the wind creates an atmosphere of excitement and adventure. Natural phenomena are used as symbols of the characters' states of mind in a manner similar to that of D.H. Lawrence.

In the European stories, on the other hand, the use of symbolism is different. It tends to be negative and expresses the drabness of city life — life spent in discussions and in cafés, full of unsolved problems, as in 'Pictures', 'Marriage à la Mode' and 'A Dill Pickle'. Even the moon symbolism in 'Bliss' has a negative quality about it, as is seen in the end of the story. In 'The Man Without a

Temperament' the use of flashbacks underlines the contrast between the life they have left behind — there is snow in London, 'You didn't expect anything else in November' (p. 337) — and the sun and foreign plants the wife delights in in the 'brilliant, dazzling garden' (p. 334). This stands in sharp contrast to the positive description of the sun in the New Zealand stories. The child narrator's world about which she writes in the New Zealand stories is one of security and basically of happiness. It would, therefore, seem that setting influences the author's approach to her narrator.

The approach to theme is very different too. One of the major themes in Katherine Mansfield's work is the polarization of man and woman, man as the time-keeper, earth bound; woman as a day-dreamer, the imaginative being, symbolized by the moon and the aloe. Examples of this polarization are to be found in the person of Bertha Young in 'Bliss', and Linda and Stanley Burnell in 'Prelude', or by comparing the first-person narrator in 'A Married Man's Story', who has a wife who understands him, with that of the singer in 'Mr Reginald Peacock's Day'. In the New Zealand stories male/female relationships as seen in the Burnells, though polarized, admit of some form of compatibility, whereas in the European stories these relationships seem to end in a state of hopelessness. A comparison of Mouse in *'Je ne parle pas français'* — who, unable to speak French, is abandoned in Paris — with Mr Hammond in 'The Stranger' — whose expectations on his wife's homecoming are shattered — shows the 'epiphany' in the French story as having a tone of finality which is not present in 'The Stranger', although the relationship will be different after what has happened.

Another dominant theme in the New Zealand stories is that of the relationship between children and parents. Here setting inevitably dictates theme. Children and parents have no place in her European stories, which, for the most part, deal only with independent adult life. Much Edwardian literature deals with parent-child relationships, but in Katherine Mansfield they are presented from the perspective of a female child who is not so much rebelling as attempting to adjust her ideas and beliefs about her purpose in life to those of her family. They are full of the child's philosophical reflections on the meaning of life, as, for example, when Laura visits the dead man in the cottage. A child's attempt to understand grown-up behaviour should, it seems to me, be a key issue in any interpretation of 'The Garden Party'.

E. Svendsen's psychoanalytical study of some of her stories[8] — based on Horney and Sullivan's conception of anxiety — has shown remarkable resemblances between Katherine Mansfield's presentation of adult women such as Linda and Beryl, and her treatment of young girls. Typical are the scenes of rejection of the child by the mother — see Linda's attitude at the beginning of 'Prelude', or the strategy of Laura's mother in 'The Garden Party'.

The feminist and psychological characteristics of Katherine Mansfield's approach as exemplified by the parent-child stories are more fully developed in some of the European stories, in particular, her 'dame seule' stories. 'The Little Governess' is a Beryl removed from the security of family life and surroundings. Miss Ross in 'Pictures' shows what happens to the artist who cannot make it and has to end by selling her body instead of her voice.

In her last two New Zealand stories Katherine Mansfield unites the techniques and themes of the European stories in a New Zealand setting. In three pages 'The Canary', an interior monologue by a 'dame seule', brings out in a most sympathetic manner the loneliness of the individual and the necessity for love. Setting no longer influences narrative; it *is* the narrative. In the unfinished 'A Married Man's Story' she combines the scenic presentation typical of the New Zealand stories with the use of a male narrator, interior monologue and epiphany. Thus, in these last stories Katherine Mansfield has reached a form which, had she lived longer, might have given us several masterpieces.

A comparison between Katherine Mansfield's background and that of her contemporary Edwardian young adult woman may explain the difference in the influence of the setting in her work. She had been brought up in a world more mid-Victorian than Edwardian. From the 1880s her middle-class British contemporaries had been reading magazines in which there were articles on jobs for young ladies and careers for women, on suffragettes and emancipation; to take some kind of further education and work was considered by her contemporaries as useful and necessary in a society where there was a shortage of men. Katherine Mansfield's economic independence allowed her the privilege of escapism, which is reflected in her writing by the emphasis on the instability of life and love. She was writing for the most part during and after a war which had far-reaching social consequences, and at a time when, like other authors, she felt it was her task as an artist to search for new forms of expression.

The artificiality found in her European stories is a result of the feeling, often mentioned in her letters and journal, that many literary people — of her age and in the world in which she moved — were trying to live in a vacuum and with false values which her own Beauchamp parentage and background could never quite accept. This is not the case in the New Zealand stories and this is what gives them their specific characteristics: a place of shared values and shared scenery, as well as the use of a child narrator and the theme of parent-child relationship which not only influences but actually determines the narrative technique.

NOTES

1. D.M. Davin writes 'it would be provincial of us, if not parochial, to claim that Katherine Mansfield learnt her art anywhere but in Europe' in W. Walsh, *Readings in Commonwealth Literature* (Oxford: Clarendon Press, 1973), p. 97.

2. *Journal of Katherine Mansfield*, edited by John Middleton Murry (London: Constable, 1954), p. 37.

3. *Letters and Journals* of Katherine Mansfield, edited by C.K. Stead (Harmondsworth: Penguin, 1977), p. 67.

4. *Journal*, p. 273.

5. *Letters and Journals* , pp. 65-66.

6. Letter to Dorothy Brett, 11 October 1917, in *Collected Letters of Katherine Mansfield*, edited by Vincent O'Sullivan and Margaret Scott, vol. 1 (Oxford: Clarendon Press, 1984), p. 331.

7. M.C. Bradbrook, 'Distance Looks our Way' in W. Walsh, *Readings in Commonwealth Literature* , pp. 114-116.

8. E. Svendsen, *Insecure Children and Anxious Women. An Analysis of Some of Katherine Mansfield's Female Characters from a Psychological Point of View* (M.A. Thesis, University of Bergen, 1987).

The Remembered Gardens Where Writing Wells: An Exploration of Katherine Mansfield's Work.

CLAUDETTE SARLET

The reading process itself has now become a major concern for critics.[1] But before turning to our reading of Katherine Mansfield's work, I would like to refer to the lesson developed by her contemporary, Marcel Proust.

This lesson has so often been used as authoritative evidence that it requires some preliminary clarification. Proust was, as we know, fiercely against Sainte-Beuve's method

> which consists in not distinguishing between the writer and his work
> ... in gathering as much information as possible on the man, collating his letters, interviewing those who knew him . . . ; this method disregards what a somewhat deeper knowledge of ourselves tells us: a book is written by another self than the one that comes to the fore in our habits, our social life, our vices.[2]

The last sentence is often quoted out of context in order to emphasize that the author of an art work is another self than the self who lives in society. While this way of using the quotation is not completely wrong, it is unduly restrictive. True, Proust was undoubtedly writing about his personal experience around 1905-1908: his deep yet at the time unrealized *wish* to become a creative writer. But we must read further and be aware that *literally* his position is that of a *reader*.

> We can only try to apprehend that different self if we turn inside and try to recreate it within our own selves. Nothing must distract from this labour in our hearts. It is a truth that we have to make up and it is too easy to believe that it will be delivered by post on a fine morning under the guise of an unpublished letter that one of our librarian-friends will have sent on, or that we will collect it from the testimony of someone who had been intimate with the author.

After establishing the existence of that 'other *self*' which creates the book and can only be the writer's self, Proust, in the rest of his essay, refers to the *reader*'s heart as the place where the work finds its truth.

Reader-writer, writer-reader, creator in becoming, Proust was attempting to save his future work from a reductive reading that would rest on social images of the 'petit Marcel', a snob and a homosexual. He himself, however, helped to spread this legend within a literary world ever eager to crystallize rumours into myths. Moreover, the complexity of the narrative structure of *A la recherche* (a story told by a first-person narrator whose first name happens to be Marcel) has favoured, if not induced, readings that tend to confuse work and life.[3]

In the case of Proust the time of such distortions seems to be over; but Katherine Mansfield's work is still too often read as transmuted life. Living as she was in avant-garde literary circles, she played the part of the fiercely independent young woman, at times outrageously eccentric in post-Victorian England, and later, during her tragically wandering last years, she bequeathed to John Middleton Murry abundant material for the golden legend he duly devised, with a choice niche in it set aside for himself.[4]

In Katherine Mansfield's case hagiography has too long taken precedence over the work itself: like any life of a saint, her legend has been used and misused in battles and for causes that have little to do with religion — or literature. Katherine Mansfield's *cause*, her first and final cause, is the necessity to write. It was the cause of her life, the cause of our readings, the cause of the continuing quest for a truth that was hers and is consonant with our intimate truth as readers who are ready to try and 'make it up' within ourselves, willing, perhaps even predisposed, to undertake this 'labour in our hearts'.

***

First a few words to avoid misunderstandings. When writers lean extensively on their own lives and particularly when they only thinly disguise the biographical material, their writings are often said to be 'autobiographical'. But saying that a novel or a short story is autobiographical can easily be a source of confusion, and we must return to the definition of autobiography as a specific narrative form.

As a genre, an autobiography is the retrospective prose story of the life of an individual told by himself. It is distinct from memoirs, which focus on the individual's public life, in that it is essentially concerned with the narrator's private life.

From the point of view of the narrative structure the classic autobiographical pattern as it was established by Rousseau[5] is characterized by a chronological retrospective ordering. At a given moment in his or her life, the nature and circumstances of which are often developed as an incipit, the narrator looks back and takes stock. This recapitulation of the past aims at giving a meaning to his life, at justifying himself, as in the case of Rousseau, or, as with Stendhal, at answering the 'Who am I?' question. The story begins with the narrator's birth and covers the whole or part of her or his life so far.

This classic pattern is still very much in use in the cheaply commercial way the genre is exploited today. In that area of popular production it is very close to the life story, to the interview, sometimes even to biography or the supposedly biographical or autobiographical novel. [6]

In France the classic pattern, thus cheapened by excessive use, has been deconstructed by writers working within the limited sphere of truly creative literature. This subversive endeavour has branched off into different directions. One such possible diversion consists in disturbing the chronological order and in introducing an element of doubt as to the narrator's identity, as is done by the 'nouveaux romanciers' — see Alain Robbe-Grillet's *Le miroir qui revient* (1984). Other authors develop a form of writing based on fragments which either are connected by verbal or notional associations, as in Michel Leiris' *La règle du jeu* (4 vols, 1948-1976), or arbitrarily follow the alphabetical order, as in *Roland Barthes par Roland Barthes* (1975).

Whatever the craftiness with which the classic pattern may be subverted, the *formal* hallmark of autobiography is the identity of author, narrator and protagonist.[7]

Consequently, whether we are referring to the classic pattern of autobiography or to modernist experiments in the form, there is not one single text in the whole of Katherine Mansfield's writing that can be said to belong to the autobiographical genre. The *Journal* lacks the retrospective dimension and thus falls within the province of the diarist practice while her correspondence belongs to the category of letter writing. If we now turn to her short stories, no textual features allow the reader to identify Kezia, for instance, with young Kathleen, or the Burnell and Sheridan families with the Beauchamp household.

I have developed these now obvious distinctions at some length because they do not seem all that obvious within the field of Mansfieldian studies. I might simply have quoted the item on autobiography in the *Encyclopedia Britannica*, for it is strikingly appropriate to our topic:

> autobiography [is] . . . the account of an individual human life, written by the subject himself. In the broadest sense any self-written account of one's life and times may be thought of as autobiographical, but autobiography as a literary genre stands apart from certain related forms — notably the personal essay, the diary, the travel journal and the autobiographical novel.

***

To read in the way Proust advocates means to read with the wish to write; to read with the dim impression that we are able to recognize the place where the writer's desire springs and wells; to uncover, in the finished work, the trails and expanses where that desire to write once roamed. For the writer sketches and etches, delineates and adumbrates as fictional representations, descriptions of places and landscapes fully integrated into the textual warp, the particular locus where his writing wells and from which his creativity springs. It can be a place, or several places, or metaphorical and imaginary positions or postures, with necessarily blurred outlines.

Finally, all critical positivists notwithstanding, to read always means to approach a text with a subjectivity that has been fed by personal experience and by books one has read, loved and made one's own.

In my own development as a reader, for instance, it is Chateaubriand's figure of the cenobite which first arrested my mind.

> On the Panama isthmus in America the Cenobite can, from the highest point in his monastery, see the two shores of the New World simultaneously: one is often stirred when the other one is at rest, and so they offer to his meditations the double picture of quiet and storm.[8]

That cenobite contemplating the 'double picture of quiet and storm' while standing on a 'narrow portion of land, enclosed on each side by water, and connecting two larger bodies of land', is a surprising metaphor for the I which is at once subject and object of *Mémoires d'Outre-Tombe*.[9] This metaphor, like others, suggests what I have called 'the outsider position of writing':[10] it was the only position possible for Chateaubriand, rent apart as he was by all the divisions between before and after the 1789 Revolution.

Later, in Marguerite Duras's *L'Amant*,[11] I visualized the imaginary place of writing as spread on the vast watery expanse of the Mekong River, which the young girl crosses again and again, between the maternal shore and the shore of her lover.[12] Through successive touches, Duras describes the fifteen-and a half year old girl. 'C'est la traversée du fleuve' (p. 16). Under the eyes of her Chinese lover, the child feels that she is becoming a woman and a writer: 'Je veux écrire' (p. 29). Sexual desire and the desire to write develop simultaneously, at the moment of separation from her mother. The realized writer includes thus in the texture of the story the imaginary place of her birth as a writing subject.

***

Like Chateaubriand or Duras, Katherine Mansfield is divided between before and after, innerly wounded by nostalgia for the lost paradise of childhood.

The years she spent at Queen's College in London with her sisters (1903-1906) were not a real break. She went back to Wellington and did not break away from her family and birthplace until she decided to leave New Zealand for good and to settle in England.

She reached London on 27 August 1908 and by 21 December she was writing in her *Journal*:

> I should like to write a life much in the style of Walter Pater's *Child in the House*. About a girl in Wellington; the singular charm and barrenness of that place — with climatic effects — wind, rain, spring, night — the sea, the cloud pageantry. And then to leave the place and go to Europe. To live there a dual existence — to go back and be utterly disillusioned, to find out the truth of all — to return to London — to live there an existence so full and strange that life itself seemed to greet her — and ill to the point of death return to W. and die there. A story — no, it would be a sketch, hardly that, more a psychological study — of the most erudite character — I should fill it with climatic disturbance — and also of the strange longing for the artificial. I should call it *Strife* — and the child I should call — ah, I have it — I'd make her a halfcaste Maori and call her Maata. (pp. 37-38)

'Halfcaste': to be both English and Maori, to sail between Wellington and London, then to return and die in Wellington. 'Halfcaste': to be neither English nor Maori, for the halfcaste really belongs to neither of her parent communities. 'Halfcaste': the arresting phantasm of belonging to two peoples, of a self divided between two origins, of the desire to realize the fusion in one's body and to be the outcome of the union of two ancestors, one of which is imaginary and represents her love for her native land.

Katherine Mansfield never returned to Wellington. After much wandering she died in Fontainebleau in a community of uprooted people.

Towards the end of her life, particularly in January 1922, she was writing down dreams of sea voyages in her *Journal*, often of journeys back to New Zealand:

> *January* 1 I dreamed I sailed to Egypt with Grandma — a very white boat. (p. 279)

> *January* 5 A long typical boat dream. I was, as usual, going to N. Z. (p. 281)

> *January* 7 I dreamed a long dream. Chummie was young again, so was Jeanne. Mother was alive. (pp. 282-283)

> *January* 14: Dreamed last night I was in a ship, with the most superb, unearthly (in the heavenly sense) seas breaking. Deep, almost violet blue waves with high foamy crests, and this white foam bore down on the blue in long curls. It was a marvellous sight. The dream was about Chummie. (p. 286)

Again and again vessels, steamers and sailing ships cross her stories and the entries in her *Journal*; they are set on more or less conscious deep-sea voyages similar to the weeks-long sailings across the Pacific and the Atlantic oceans.

Her second and most painful severance was the death of Chummie, the little brother who had just brought to London large gusts of childhood, of light and air from her native country. Now that we are aware of the importance psychological factors may have in the development of illnesses such as tuberculosis, we know that this separation, which would for ever be impossible to acknowledge, may have contributed to the consumption she started suffering from in 1917.

Leslie was killed on 7 October 1915. On 29 October she wrote in her *Journal*:

> I believe in immortality because he is not here, and I long to join him. (p. 86)

In November at Bandol she also noted:

> I am just as much dead as he is . . . why don't I commit suicide? Because I feel I have a duty to perform to the lovely time when we were both alive. (pp. 89-90)

Memories crowd into the pages of her *Journal*, of gardens and trees, of noises and smells:

> *Evening.*
> *October* They are walking up and down the garden in Acacia Road. It is dusky; the Michaelmas daisies are bright as feathers. From the old fruit-tree at the bottom of the garden — the slender tree rather like a poplar — there falls a little round pear, hard as a stone.
> 'Did you hear that, Katie! Can you find it? By Jove — that familiar sound.' (p. 83)

This splendid dialogue of remembrance goes on, both dreamt and written down, so that life becomes stronger than death:

> 'we were almost like one child. . . . I remembered ruffling the violet leaves with you — Oh, that garden!' . . .
> 'We shall go back there one day — when it's all over.'
> 'We'll go back together.'
> 'And find everything —'
> 'Everything!' (pp. 84-5)

In November at Bandol, just before mentioning suicide, she wrote:

> 'Do you remember, Katie?' I hear his voice in the trees and flowers, in scents and light and shadow. (p. 89)

These extracts from her *Journal* are like landmarks (or seamarks) pointing towards gardens as the selected places where some of her best stories found their roots, stories such as 'Bliss', 'Prelude' or 'At the Bay'.

The pear tree in 'Bliss' is the same pear tree as the one in the English garden in Acacia Road where pears in falling make the same noise as those of Tinaki Road, Wellington. Compare the *Journal*: 'the *slender* tree rather like a poplar' (p. 83, my italics) with 'Bliss': 'And the two women stood side by side looking at the *slender*, flowering tree' (p. 312, my italics).

As early as 16 February 1916 Katherine Mansfield was writing down in her *Journal* fragments and sketches of 'The Aloe', a substantial part of which already seems to have been written by that time. She anticipated that the story would conclude on a vision of the little brother in his grand-mother's arms and that the child would have to 'mean the world to Linda' (p. 98), the strange, faraway mother. This draft was to branch off into several texts: 'The Aloe' (which was published posthumously), 'Prelude' and 'At the Bay'. Only the two stories that she published during her life time will be considered here.

Katherine Mansfield's work largely proceeds from what I would call an 'aesthetics of the vacillating heart'. Most of her stories are built on a recurring pattern that falls into two moments.

First moment: two human beings, a man and a woman, or two women, are together. They communicate through their eyes and their silent presence to each other. They share an intense intimate relationship.

Second moment: a misplaced word or gesture topples the relationship from intimacy to alienation, to a sense of complete estrangement, or even to hatred.

Sometimes these two moments occur in the reverse order; sometimes they are repeated. The painful intensity to be found in many of Mansfield's stories almost always originates in such 'intermittences of the heart' that are more sudden and violent than with Proust.

This pattern is significant in that the locus of her creation, the place where writing wells, is located at the moment of intimacy or fusion.

In 'Prelude', a moment of fusion between Linda and her mother occurs when they are both looking at the aloe. Earlier in the story Kezia wanders alone in front of the unknown plant. As she sees her mother 'coming down the path', she asks her about it. Linda tells her the name of the plant and that it only flowers 'once every hundred years'. The child's fascination with the aloe, combined with what her mother has told her, gives the plant, isolated as it is on a 'high grassy bank' that looks like an island, a magical and mythical dimension. At night Linda joins her mother in the garden.

> As they stood on the steps, the high grassy bank on which the aloe rested rose up like a wave, and the aloe seemed to ride upon it like a ship with the oars lifted. Bright moonlight hung upon the lifted oars like water, and on the green wave glittered the dew.
> 'Do you feel it, too,' said Linda, and she spoke to her mother with

the special voice that women use at night to each other as though they spoke in their sleep or from some hollow cave — 'Don't you feel that it is coming towards us?' (pp. 253-254)

In the liquid moonlight there develops an intimate communion between mother and daughter, and, simultaneously, a fusion with the magic plant. But Linda dreams on:

Nobody would dare to come near the ship or to follow after. (p. 254)

This is her obsession: that no one should come near her, neither her husband, who keeps making her pregnant, nor the children, who are too heavy to bear.[13]

In 'Prelude' the alternation of love and hate is recurrent. Nothing is actually broken, nothing is big enough to fulfil Kezia's thirst for love, everything vibrates with life; the garden, the house, people, or the calico cat, repeatedly shock the child into a sense of wonder that is at times painful and at times, as with Pat's uncovered ear-ring after he has chopped off the duck's head, comforting.

Written in September 1921, i.e., five years after 'Prelude', 'At the Bay' completes, in the imaginary realm of fiction, the transition from a quest for fusion to a representation of newly discovered love between mother and child; yet here the child is his mother's son, the little brother.

The heart no longer vacillates. Beryl is the only character who is still dissatisfied with her life; but irony turns her into an eccentric figure who stands slightly apart from the family. Everything is filled with the glitter of a many-sided sense of love: love for nature (remember the opening of the story that so vividly describes the slow dawning of light through the morning mist out of which eventually emerges 'an enormous shock-haired giant', a 'big gum-tree'); Linda's love for her father, for her husband Stanley, who desires her, and whom she in fact desires too; love of the grand-mother for little Kezia, a love so true and deep that it manages to defeat in laughter the anguish the child feels at the thought that the old woman might die and leave her.

Here again, the place where plenitude is experienced is the garden, under the manuka tree. This is where Part VI takes place: Linda is reclining on a steamer chair with her baby boy on the grass beside her. Although she first wants to dismiss him as an unwanted burden, he forces upon her, through his eloquent smile, a true dialogue of love that is different from the whispering of fusion. Indeed when he has finally conquered his mother's love, he no longer even looks at her but moves on to conquer the world: to grab the soft pink thing waving in front of him.

This place, under the manuka tree, is where the shift from a state of fusion to the liberating distance of love takes place. Under the manuka tree the morbid quest for complete identification is sublimated and the dimension of genuine love between mother and child allows at last for the free play of creativity.

From 'Prelude' to 'At the Bay' Katherine Mansfield's fiction moves away from the painful pursuit of fusion, ever threatened by, and therefore alternating with, moments of hatred, and opens on to the transitional space of love.[14] In those two stories that so vividly picture her native country Katherine Mansfield presents two imaginary, almost mythical places from which her writing, and her desire to write, have welled: the steps from which mother and daughter look at the aloe as it becomes a ship sailing upon the water of moonlight and the shadow of the manuka tree in which mother and son are born to the life of love. The power of her writing she drew from those remembered gardens of childhood, from those gardens she had dedicated to her missing brother.

***

I now wish to sketch, within this commentary, the personal landscape through which Katherine Mansfield's stories have found an echo in me; I wish to delineate the imaginary space of my reading.

The reader lifts her eyes. Books by Katherine Mansfield are lying on the table. Drops from the last shower are still winding down the window pane. The river water is brownish because there has been too much rain. On the opposite bank the grass is turning yellow and the fishermen of summer have disappeared. On top of a building a neon sign already outlines its six red letters against the darkening sky: BELCAM. Above the green bar of the chestnut tree walk heavy clouds are caught by the setting sun in a pink light that turns their dark grey shades into mauves and violets: had Katherine not perceived Belgium as being green and mauve? 'I love Belgium for I love green & mauve.'[15]

Staring at those gaping pages and at this slow drifting into the autumn night the reader confuses in her dream different skies and different landscapes, gardens, trees and flowers. She can see, more vividly than ever before, the ever rustling bulk of the huge mimosa tree at the end of the walk along the house; she can see its light silver leaves standing out against the dark greens of the surrounding tropical bushes, she can feel its small sensitive balls of yellow down, so soft to the little girl's fingers. Her dream eye lingers upon the bougainvillea that cover the roof of the house, upon their warm violet and salmon and crimson shades, then drifts to the overflowing baskets of creamy flowers propped up on the frangipani's frail limbs. And she can hear the thud of overripe mangoes falling to the ground, out there, in the garden of her own childhood, in Africa.

NOTES

1. This paper, read in French at the centenary conference, and the quotations from French works, have been translated into English by Christine Pagnoulle.

2. Marcel Proust, 'La méthode de Sainte-Beuve' in *Contre Sainte-Beuve* (Paris: Gallimard, 1954), pp. 136-137.

3. In this respect George D. Painter's biography (London: Chatto Windus; Boston: Little Brown, 1959 and 1965) is a complete betrayal of Proust as a man and as a writer. This so-called biography is merely an extensive paraphrase of *A la recherche du temps perdu*.

4. See Ian A. Gordon's paper in this collection, which gives a very clear outline of the way Katherine Mansfield's work has been perceived since its publication.

5. Autobiography as a genre illustrates with particular clarity the way in which a new literary form can emerge. For centuries there were a number of scriptural practices to which the autobiographical *form* is indebted in one way or another: confessions, family record books or diaries ('livres de raison'), chronicles, memoirs, 'lives' of saints or of famous men. Yet nothing deserved the name 'autobiography' until a text crystallized the form and founded autobiography as a genre. Rousseau's *Confessions* played this role in Europe even though English and Spanish writers had anticipated the form as early as the seventeenth or eighteenth centuries. Later the new pattern was to be used as such until new experimentation subverted it. Emergence and deconstruction of the pattern are to be related to deep socio-historical changes: the history of autobiography is closely linked with the emergence and development of the notion of the individual subject. See *Individualisme et autobiographie en Occident*, edited by Cl. Delhez-Sarlet and by M. Catani (Brussels: Editions de l'Université de Bruxelles, 1983) which outlined the parallelism between successive emergences of the 'autobiographical gesture' and the progressive formation of individualism in Western culture. On this see the work of Louis Dumont, especially *Essais sur l'individualisme* (Paris: Seuil, 1983).

    Many books have been published on autobiography. The first studies in the field were published in English; see, for instance, Wayne Shumaker, *English Autobiography. Its Emergence, Materials and Form* (Berkeley and Los Angeles: University of California Press, 1954). In France many studies have been published since 1970. Note, by Philippe Lejeune, *L'autobiographie en France* (Paris: Seuil, 1971), *Le pacte autobiographique* (Paris: Seuil, 1975), *Je est un autre/.L'autobiographie, de la littérature aux médias* (Paris: Seuil, 1980), *Moi aussi* (Paris: Seuil, 1986); Michel Beaujour, *Miroirs d'encre: Rhétorique de l'autoportrait* (1980), and Georges May,

L'autobiographie (1979). These works also provide bibliographical surveys.

6. On the effects of such close literary kinship, see Philippe Lejeune's last two book-length studies, and his essay 'Autobiographie, roman et nom propre' in *Moi aussi*.

7. Lejeune clearly defined the formal marks of the genre in *Le pacte autobiographique*. Since then he has repented this rigorously structural analysis and has moved from a rather unbending theorizing to complete empiricism. That publishers find it financially worthwhile to blur distinctions between autobiography and novel does not mean that the critic must give up trying to define as keenly as possible the specificities of each literary genre.

8. Chateaubriand, *Le génie du christianisme*, edited by M. Regard (Paris: Gallimard 'La Pléiade', 1972), p. 876.

9. Oxford English Dictionary definition for the word 'isthmus'.

10. Claudette Delhez-Sarlet, 'Chateaubriand: scissions et rassemblement du moi dans l'histoire' in *Individualisme et autobiographie en Occident*, pp. 193-208 (See note 5).

11. Marguerite Duras, *L'Amant* (Paris: Editions de Minuit, 1984).

12. Claudette Sarlet, 'D'un jardin de l'Ouelle à la traversée du Mékong. Autoportrait et sujet de l'écriture' in *Penser le sujet aujourd'hui* (Paris: Méridiens-Klincksieck, 1988), pp. 267-289.

13. Françoise Defromont's paper in this collection and conversations I had with her at the centenary conference helped to clarify my perception of Linda and of her refusal of children.

14. This passage is inspired by D.W. Winnicott, *Playing and Reality* (New-York: Basic Books, 1971). I use here the word 'transitional' to define a space, while Winnicott applies it to an object: a teddy bear can thus function as a transitional object that makes it possible for the child to leave his mother's breast.

15. Letter to Garnet Trowell, 28-30 April 1909, in *Collected Letters of Katherine Mansfield*, edited by Vincent O'Sullivan and Margaret Scott, vol. 1 (Oxford: Clarendon Press, 1984), p. 91.

SONGS OF PROTEST

Katherine Mansfield as a Noble Savage: The Cry Against Corruption

NELSON WATTIE

The words 'a cry against corruption' are familiar to readers of Katherine Mansfield as her formulation of intention in writing the story *'Je ne parle pas français'*. She goes on to clarify the meaning of her phrase by saying: 'Not a protest — a *cry*, and I mean corruption in the widest sense of the word, of course'.[1] Critical comment on Katherine Mansfield does not always make it sufficiently clear that she was not only a charming teller of tales but also a profound and rigorous thinker.[2] For all her role playing, she was uncompromising and even ruthless when it came to formulating what was most important to her — namely the basis of her art. For this reason, every word in the phrase under consideration deserves close attention.

Although it is not my present purpose, it would be possible, for example, to conduct a discussion of the difference between committed fiction or *littérature engagée* on the one hand and expressive literature on the other by analysing Katherine Mansfield's distinction between a 'protest' and a 'cry'. The former comes to us from the intellect, the latter from the sensate being of the artist. By making the distinction Katherine Mansfield is assuring us that her 'cry against corruption' does not place her among those whose writing is 'engagée'. She reinforces this by referring to 'corruption in the widest sense', since *littérature engagée* is a fiction of protest against political or social corruption in a comparatively narrow sense. What is, in fact, 'the widest sense of the word'? This question will prompt much of what follows in this paper.

But I suspect that its main title will cause more puzzlement than its subtitle. Why call Katherine Mansfield a 'noble savage'? This is a term we associate with the Enlightenment and Romanticism to suggest a claim that 'natural' man has finer qualities than 'civilized' man. Today we tend to view the concept as a fiction rather than as a realistic description of the people who came to be colonized. The 'noble savage' is an image created rather than perceived by so-called 'civilized' man, and he created it with a purpose, namely as a means to criticize the corruption of 'civilization' itself. Criticizing corrup-

149

tion — yes, the connections are becoming clearer. A 'noble savage' is a being who comes from outside the society concerned and acts as a rod by which the corruption of that society can be measured, as Katherine Mansfield entered English society from New Zealand. Many second-generation colonial novels contrast the 'natural' behaviour of the colonial-born with the effete, over-civilized behaviour of the new-comer from England. A close reading of any of the excellent Katherine Mansfield biographies will make it clear that her English contemporaries did view her as an outsider, an anomaly and even, at times, as a 'savage'. This seems to have been Hugh Kingsmill's view, and in irritable moments D.H. Lawrence shared it. However, it would be much more difficult to find English opinions that viewed Katherine Mansfield as 'noble', especially if we suspect the honesty of Middleton Murry's utterances.

It is not by chance that I have moved from the customary unitary concept of the 'noble savage' to a dualistic one which separates the quality of 'nobility' from that of 'savagery'. It is deliberate, because I want to suggest that there is a polarity in Katherine Mansfield's creative thought which can be usefully, if somewhat simplistically, labelled with these terms. In another place[3] I have pointed out the difference in tone between Katherine Mansfield's warm engaged writing in the New Zealand stories and her brittle, witty, sometimes even sarcastic writing in the stories about the English intelligentsia. This distinction is a possible starting-place for perceiving what is 'noble' and what is 'savage' in Katherine Mansfield's creative thought.

Only a starting-place however, because ultimately it will be necessary to transcend the national element in the distinction between the noble and the savage in Katherine Mansfield. To transcend it does not mean to neglect it — I am convinced that Katherine Mansfield's experiential perception of the differences between the New Zealand environment of her childhood and the English-European environment of her adulthood were at the basis of her general view of human life, but it is this general view, her *Weltanschauung,* which concerns me more at present than its analytical basis. The distinction between the noble and the savage in Katherine Mansfield's fiction has perceptible roots in the two major realms of her experience — but these are only partly geographical or national. Above all, if we do not attempt to transcend the vital national element in the distinction, we will fail to notice that the noble and the savage in Katherine Mansfield have a common feature, a common purpose, namely the 'cry against corruption'. In this cry the distinctions are transcended and merge into a common urgency. What is savage in Katherine Mansfield is her reaction to corruption; what is noble in her is the image of human dignity she creates in opposition to that corruption; both of them are to be heard in the cry that is her fiction.

When we contemplate Katherine Mansfield's emphatic remark that her fiction is a cry against corruption, we might begin by taking the term 'corruption' in some of its obvious and most conventional meanings. We tend to associate it first with power politics and financial manipulation, but such concerns are rarely Katherine Mansfield's. When she claimed that literature after the First World War should be quite different from that before it, she mocked the idea that it must be concerned with 'mobilisation and the violation of Belgium'[4] and I believe we would be justified in placing political and economic corruption on the same phenomenal level as these. They may well be the *causes* of a change in consciousness, but it is the *nature* of consciousness itself that is her concern. This is implied by what she says next in the same letter: 'I feel in the *profoundest* sense that things can never be the same'. Compare this 'profoundest sense' with the 'widest sense' in which she claims to speak of corruption and one sees that the superlatives are an effort to reach towards something beyond the rim of the sayable.

There are however ways of saying the unsayable; in fact this is what all the arts aim at doing. Before pursuing this thought further, it will help to look at examples of corruption that Katherine Mansfield does supply and that stand between the crudest level of definition we have just dismissed and the profounder, wider level that Katherine Mansfield seems to mean. I am thinking now of the corruption that is manifested in the abuse of advantage and privilege in human affairs, derived from differences in social class, income, gender, age and the like. 'The Garden Party', 'The Doll's House' and 'Life of Ma Parker' all offer moving examples of the corruption inherent in social class. In the opening part of 'The Garden Party' Laura realizes that she cannot make the imaginative leap across the gap between the workers and herself. 'What was he thinking?' she asks herself of one, and when we read 'Oh, how extraordinarily nice the workmen were, she thought', we realize that she genuinely wants to bridge the gap, but is blocked by that patronizing concept 'nice'. The final phase of the story, when Laura visits the workmen's cottages, reveals the acute pain in the awareness of her own incapacity to sympathize, symbolized by her unsuitable hat, and it is clear that such pain can only be avoided in one of two ways. One of these is to ignore the gap and make no effort to bridge it; this way is chosen by Laura's mother who is able to sustain her cheerfulness by remaining callous and indifferent towards the unhappy workmen and their families. The other way is to make a supreme act of the empathetic imagination and to 'become' the other. This is achieved by no character in the story, but it is what Laura aims at and fails to accomplish. It is however achieved by the author and the narrator and it is what is meant in Katherine Mansfield's famous theoretical comment where she says that if she writes of a duck she becomes a duck.[5] Complete indifference or complete empathy are ways to escape the pain of ineffective sympathy, but the former is a manifestation of corruption, and the cry of 'The Garden Party' is clearly directed against it, just as it is directed against the adults of 'The Doll's House' and the 'literary gentleman' of 'Life of Ma Parker'. The central characters of both these stories demonstrate the empathy which dissolves corruption and which therefore deserves our attention: it is one part of what is 'noble' in Katherine Mansfield.

'The Doll's House' shows not only ignorance and corruption dividing social classes but also those same qualities dividing generations. There are many other stories which do this, notably those that so famously show Katherine Mansfield's skill in depicting children, but also those like 'Miss Brill' and 'Pictures' which demonstrate discrimination against the ageing. I shall leave others to point out the stories in which corruption is a matter of gender, but I feel the need to point out to those others that privileges of gender are only one example, neither more nor less important or meaningful than the already quoted examples of corruption through privilege and underprivilege of other kinds.

In fact we must go further than this and make it clear that none of these forms of corruption is 'corruption in the widest sense'. At best they are metaphors or metonymic illustrations of that widest and profoundest corruption that provokes Katherine Mansfield's cry. Let me leap over some links in the chain of argument, which we shall take up again immediately, in order to make it clear where we are heading: the corruption that causes Katherine Mansfield to cry out is the corruption of the cosmos itself.

In recent years much has been written of Katherine Mansfield's debt to Symbolism and in that discussion useful new insights into her work have been acquired. But it seems to me that too little has been made of the philosophical pessimism which underlies Symbolism and which underlies Katherine Mansfield's creative and critical thought. We can trace the chain of influence back through Symbolism to the greatest philosophical pessimist of them all: to Arthur Schopenhauer. Schopenhauer made a deep and lasting impression on Baudelaire, in conjunction with Wagner's music and thought, which is in turn profoundly shaped by his reading of Schopenhauer. Through Baudelaire these thoughts were transmitted to the French Symbolists and to their followers in many nations. Furthermore scholarship never tires of tracing Friedrich Nietzsche's pervasive influence on modernism, and that his philosophy is a re-formulation, extension and illustration of Schopenhauer's thought is something Nietzsche himself gladly admitted. I have found no reference to Schopenhauer in Katherine Mansfield's writings, but his influence, direct and indirect, was so pervasive during her life-time that she would not have had to read him in order to absorb it. Furthermore her own experience of life could lead her independently to similar conclusions. Finally, it is worth noting that her friend D.H. Lawrence read Schopenhauer with great excitement during his college years.[6]

Central to Schopenhauer's thought is the perception that human suffering is inevitable because it is endemic to the nature of humanity and the world. It is not surprising that he came to admire the writings of Buddhist thinkers when he discovered that they shared his awareness of the inevitability of suffering, and like them too he also believed that there are strategies for avoiding the inevitable, if only temporarily. One such strategy is that practised by mystics, another is that practised by the greatest artists, and clearly it is this second strategy that is of relevance here.

Briefly, the reason for mankind's suffering lies in the physical limitations of our existence and our awareness distinguishes humanity from the objects and living things that share existence. All existence is bound into a chain of cause and effect within a spatial and temporal frame. Our awareness of this chain and the energy of our will — this will being nothing less than the chain of cause and effect as it acts within us - leads to a yearning for escape from the chain. Our bodies can, in fact, never escape, but our minds can do so in moments of mystic or aesthetic contemplation.

The act of aesthetic contemplation in this framework is an act of perception released from the needs, urges, wishes, hopes, desires, in fact from the contingent being of the perceiver. In our customary bondage to the inevitable chain of cause and effect, which is our inner corruption, we see what we want to see: we see what satisfies our needs and fears. In the moment of aesthetic awareness we see what is there, independent of its and our bondage in the (nonetheless inevitably continuing) chain of cause and effect. This is why we say of such moments: 'I was taken out of myself', 'I lost all sense of time', 'I forgot where I was' — we are mentally, though not physically, liberated from the restraints of time and place and therefore, however fleetingly, from the inevitability of suffering.

That Katherine Mansfield experienced such liberation from her own dreadful suffering when writing is witnessed by her theoretical comments on the aesthetics of empathy: that she becomes a duck when writing of a duck, that, putatively, her friend Brett becomes an apple when painting an apple.

> In fact this whole process of becoming the duck (what Lawrence would, perhaps, call this "consummation with the duck or the apple") is so thrilling that I can hardly breathe, only to think about it. For although that is as far as most people can get, it is really only the 'prelude'. There follows the moment when you are *more* duck, *more* apple or *more* Natasha than any of these objects could ever possibly be, and so you create them anew. 7

Each story of Katherine Mansfield offers the reader an opportunity to share such a moment of liberation. It is less common, however, for characters within the stories to be so privileged, although we might remember children such as Sun in 'Sun and Moon' when he sees the 'nut for a handle' on the ice pudding, or Kezia and the Kelveys when they see the little lamp in the doll's house. And we might remember the 'corruption' which surrounds and endangers such 'noble' moments, provoking the narrator's 'savage' anger.

Or we might remember Bertha Young's similarly endangered moment of perception when she gazes at the pear tree in 'Bliss'. This story does as well as any other to illustrate those qualities in Katherine Mansfield's creative thought which I have labelled - clumsily, perhaps - 'savagery' and 'nobility'. The 'bliss' that Bertha feels is a vital, surging, subtle energy; although she is thirty it is like the burgeoning passion of the adolescent girl in 'The Wind Blows'. It is potentially aesthetic and potentially sexual, it is will and it is libido, but it exceeds any of the objects that are available to satisfy it and is therefore endangered; it is potential suffering. She wants to expend it on her baby, but the Nanny warns her: 'Now, don't excite her after her supper. You know you do, M'm. And I have such a time with her after!'. She offers it to her husband, who says on the telephone: 'Look here. I'll be late. I'll take a taxi and come along as quickly as I can, but get dinner put back ten minutes — will you?'.

There is potential for satire here but Katherine Mansfield reserves that for Bertha's house-guests. Their affectations, their social masks, their meaningless language, their absurd sense of values, their inability to sympathize with others, let alone empathize, the poverty of their feelings and the weakness of their thought combined with their vanity — all these things provoke Katherine Mansfield's 'savagery'. These parts of the story are pitilessly satirical, but before we accuse Katherine Mansfield of cruelty, of abandoning her own nobility, we should consider that all these objects of satirical fury are examples of humans yielding to the inevitability of their own suffering, making no effort to escape the bondage of selfishness, or better, of self. And then Miss Fulton and Bertha, who are rivals and potential enemies, move towards a moment of escape from the chain of suffering. Amongst other things it is signalled by a growing stillness. Miss Fulton speaks in a 'cool, sleepy voice', and we might be reminded that when Sun saw the nut 'he felt quite tired and had to lean against Cook'.

We should not see such 'sleepiness' as a subsidence of the 'blissful' energy, but rather as a sign that it has found a satisfying object, so that there is a suspension of the driving, restless force of suffering will. When the Kelvey sisters saw the little lamp, they 'had forgotten the cross lady. . . . Then both were silent once more'. In the moment of contemplation Bertha and Miss Fulton are also silent, and their sense of time and space is suspended:

> How long did they stand there? Both, as it were, caught in that circle of unearthly light, understanding each other perfectly, creatures of another world, and wondering what they were to do in this one with all this blissful treasure that burned in their bosoms and dropped, in silver flowers, from their hair and hands? ('Bliss', pp. 312-13)

The tone of satire has vanished. Katherine Mansfield is no longer 'savage' but 'noble'; and yet the two styles merge almost imperceptibly into one unified story. They are, in fact, two aspects of one aesthetic act. They are both parts of that 'cry against corruption' that is Katherine Mansfield's fiction. The savagery is necessary for the imaging of corruption, the nobility is necessary for imaging its opposite, and taken together they make of Katherine Mansfield, in the widest and profoundest sense of the term, 'a noble savage'.

NOTES

1. Letter to John Middleton Murry, 3 February 1918, in *The Collected Letters of Katherine Mansfield,* edited by Vincent O'Sullivan with Margaret Scott, vol. 2 (Oxford: Clarendon Press, 1987), p. 54.

2. A critic who shows a lively awareness of Katherine Mansfield as a creative thinker is Kate Fullbrook. I am indebted to many of her insights in *Katherine Mansfield* (Brighton: The Harvester Press, 1986) but believe that she artificially reduces the range of their validity by squeezing them into a 'feminist' funnel.

3. Nelson Wattie, *Nation und Literatur: Eine Studie zur Bestimmung der nationalen Merkmale literarischer Werke am Beispiel von Katherine Mansfields Kurzgeschichten* (Bonn: Bouvier, 1980).

4. Letter to John Middleton Murry, 10 November 1919, in *Katherine Mansfield's Letters to John Middleton Murry: 1913-1922,* edited by John Middleton Murry (London: Constable, 1951), p. 380.

5. Letter to Dorothy Brett, 11 October 1917, in *The Collected Letters of Katherine Mansfield*, edited by Vincent O'Sullivan & Margaret Scott, vol. 1 (Oxford: Clarendon Press, 1984), p. 330.

6. See Harry T. Moore, *The Priest of Love: A Life of D.H. Lawrence* (revised edition, Harmondsworth: Penguin, 1976), pp. 111-112.

7. See note 5.

Impossible Mourning

FRANÇOISE DEFROMONT

Written as they are in an elusive style that relies on impressionistic touches, Katherine Mansfield's short stories radiate an atmosphere of light and lightness. Yet underneath this aerial world the inexorable sweep of the sickle of death can be perceived. Katherine Mansfield, like Dorothy Richardson,[1] is one of those women writers who have included in their writings the reality, and indeed the haunting questions, of death. Death recurs in her stories as some secret obsession, very often as the death of a child perceived by women. Her approach is deep and sharp, for she probes the deeper layers of their inner selves as she confronts her women protagonists not so much with death itself as with its refracted shadows on their identities.

Such insights are revealed with the utmost violence, but only for fleeting moments that can easily be overlooked when reading her stories. Beneath the smooth surface her vision is sharp to the point of cruelty because she regards death as an everlasting scandal. What she centres on is the aspect of suffering that is most difficult to accept, and therefore most often occulted.

However, just as she is about to reach the farthest and darkest limit, something is withheld. This made me wonder what hidden disruption was thus suddenly disclosed — as if in such textual moments something was checked by a boundary impossible to trespass. This is why I felt the need to penetrate beneath the surface and explore those instances in the text where, at the moment of loss, something retreats and retracts, leaving the reader with an annihilating sense of impossibility.

Starting from the most obvious asperity in the text, namely the connection between the identity of the woman and the loss of her love-object, I shall try to understand why the unbearable confrontation with death leads to reversal effects in the text. Eventually I will try to show how the escape movement is related to an 'impossible mourning'.

There is something almost like a scream in several short stories. Striking similarities can be found in the stories based on the dual relationship between a woman and a love-object, whether a child, a young man, or even a bird, as in 'Life of Ma Parker', 'Millie' and 'The Canary', respectively. To these three stories I wish to add 'Miss Brill', for reasons that will become apparent later.

The first of these stories brings out the basic reference pattern of the mother-child relationship as exemplified by Ma Parker and Lennie; this painful and very real loss reappears, though under different forms, in each story. 'Millie', for example, deals with the encounter between a lonely woman and a young man who bears the stamp of death, for he has killed and has in fact already been sentenced to death by those who mean to take their revenge on him.

Lennie's fate in 'Life of Ma Parker' and the bird's in 'The Canary' are entwined with the two women who love them; these women are alike both in their sufferings and because of their social background. However, a shift has occurred, since the canary seems to be a substitute and can thus be considered as a metaphor for a real child.

This interpretation is confirmed, I think, by the close connection that links together child and animal in 'The Voyage', where the presence of a living child summons up a bestiary imbued with the magic of Alice's wonderland. Fenella's 'voyage' takes her to the land of childhood, to a world that is not unlike that of Snow-White and the Seven Dwarfs, as suggested by the miniature setting and the metaphors, as well as by the atmosphere created by a little horse, the appearance of a white cat that unfolds like a camel, and a bird-like grandfather. The most significant symbol in a childhood thus brought to life by the child's own fantasy is her grandmother's swan-necked umbrella that has to be carried unbroken to the end of the voyage, just as the little girl herself is taken by her grandmother away from a world of gloom towards another land where a bird-like Santa Claus is lying in a bed — a world which is the umbrella's final destination. The umbrella that must be protected and kept unbroken represents a childhood shielded from death and peopled with live animals. It is a metaphor of the child as a love-object, or as a fetish-object, creating some kind of magic circle round Fenella, who is thus protected from death by her own imaginary world.

Another character, Miss Brill, is also associated with a fetish-object — her fur — no longer a living animal but an inanimate object, a fossilized scarf. What is presented here is the very opposite of what is described in 'Life of Ma Parker', for it shows a woman in her neurotic relationship with a love-object which she has invested with her fantasies, a fetish artificially substituted for the other, absent loved one[2] — whether a man, her own sexual self, or a child. In comparison with the reference pattern mentioned above, i.e., the actual loss of a child, this is the ultimate stage in a decomposition process where the love-object has become a dead fetish and where the identity of the woman is fragmenting. Nothing remains alive, not even her suffering, for the woman who is clinging to her shrivelled love-object buries her last cry of agony with it.

It is by presenting the sense of loneliness that suddenly overwhelms them that Katherine Mansfield discloses the gap that furrows the identity of women: 'It is the loneliness which is so appalling' (p. 345), says Monica in 'Revelations'. They experience utter despair: 'How I loved him! Perhaps it does not matter so very much what it is one loves in this world' ('The Canary', p. 539). Indeed it hardly matters whether what is loved is a child, a canary, or a fur; what is highlighted is the relationship to an object, and consequently the relationship to the other as object. The disappearance of the object threatens with destruction the very identity of the subject, which thus becomes a crucial issue. The emptiness outlined in these texts gives them a double metaphysical edge insofar as the ontological question of the subject is presented in a love relationship to an object. Moreover, the face-to-face encounter with the absolute absence of love is here written out as confrontation with the absolute absence of object. The protagonist is confronted with the void of nothingness, or of the other (of the others, as Sartre would put it), not as a form of hell, but as sheer nothingness. This is a ruthless and cruel vision where the vanishing of the object unavoidably implies the vanishing of the subject. This is why Miss Brill's confrontation with the object as nothingness in its abysmal nudity drives her towards a symbolical death: the loss of her last illusion about the other — which can no longer exist, even as a fantasy — leads to the woman's entombment in the wake of her fetishized object. I see this as the subtle transcription of a psychic death process.

The identity of the subject faced with that disappearance comes apart, and consequently, as can be seen in 'Revelation', a minor yet significant story, there is no central locus where grief can be held together in the inner self, for the subject-object relationship has been cut open with nothingness and has shattered to pieces even the suffering self. In this short story, the young woman is tormented by a vague but terrible anguish that reflects the death of a child, which will be disclosed later, and is refracted through the three main characters. 'Madame', who, though this is not specified, might be the child's mother, bears the stigmata of sorrow in her red and swollen eyes, whereas the father, who is explicitly named as such and should thus be the sufferer, is like a wooden man with a paper face, as if removed from his body by unexpressed grief. Monica, who has no connection with their lives, weeps in their stead as if her tears were deprived of their actual source and could not spring from a meaningful self. Sorrow thus seems to split into scattered fragments; it is cut off from its roots in the identity of the subject involved, and therefore is deprived of itself to the point of becoming meaningless. Nothingness and meaninglessness, these are the dead-ends to which Katherine Mansfield's approach to death leads. Actual death and death of the soul both point to an unbearable suffering and the implicit revolt it prompts in the sufferer's heart. Though death is not explicitly presented as scandalous, the impression of scandal is clearly generated by a number of textual effects: indeed the obsessively recurring question of death associated with a child produces 'text reversals', which I shall now look at.

When Kezia lies in her beloved grandmother's arms for an afternoon nap, the very moment of closest proximity is suddenly rent apart by the shadow of separation i.e., with the child's first fleeting awareness of death. In other stories the shadow of death appears only in filigree, as is the case with Fenella's mother. Here the confrontation between a living child and death leads to a volte-face in the story, for Fenella's voyage consists in leaving the grim space of death to go 'elsewhere', towards light and dawn, towards a wonderful world, the world of 'marvellous' childhood untouched by death.[3] This 'elsewhere' opens a door to the child's own imaginary land which in turn includes her perception of death. The gloom connected with the deceased thus fades out as if in a dream and melts into a dream-like texture, a little horse, a white cat and a miniature shell house... but something reappears all of a sudden as a big black frame painted by the grandmother — a 'text', writes Katherine Mansfield — that reminds us of a death notification seen by the little girl in her

previous life and sadly echoing from afar. The announcement '*Lost!
... It Is* GONE FOR EVER!' ('The Voyage', p. 476) ironically seems to play with death and deny it, for the heart of childhood is not rent in two by this inscription which quivers as if in strange suspense. Doesn't this convey children's way of coming to terms with death, making it a part of their games as if they could trespass insuperable limits with the lightest freedom of movement? It is a quivering suspense between dream and reality, between irrevocable loss and the wholeness of 'marvellous' childhood, between life and death, for a fleeting instant — the fleeting wink of a grandfather Christmas drawn from a fairy tale, as if a strange and yet familiar recollection was just vanishing...

However, beyond the extremely delicate perceptiveness of Katherine Mansfield, idealized childhood appears as a counterpoint to death in 'The Voyage', as if the confrontation of the live child with death entailed a textual wheeling about reverting towards a place outside time, i.e., childhood protected from death thanks to its power of dreaming out the world.

Yet the same confrontation produces opposite effects in other short stories where violence is rounded on itself with a most destructive impact. Such reversals then point to a paroxysm of violence, including infanticide.

In 'The Child-Who-Was-Tired',[4] the most explicit example, the theme of child and death is double since the infanticide committed by the little girl, who is no more than a child herself, draws her towards her own death through 'a little road that led to nowhere, and where nobody walked at all' (p. 22). 'Nowhere' and 'nobody' point to death as once more connected with stark loneliness, as in 'Miss Brill'. Moreover the structure of this short story involving two children calls to mind the idea of a guilty self splitting into two, one facing the other, and thus expressing a sense of destruction. Psychic death is again brought about by the abyss of utmost loneliness engulfing the murderous child and shatters her identity, as though the death of her soul was the expression of her boundless guilt.

The approach is the same in 'The Fly' where the collapse of the boss's deeper self is performed through oblivion. The murder of the fly has something to do with that of his beloved son, for they are both innocent victims; the boss kills the fly in order to obliterate his own suffering, as if he was actually killing his wound — or even his own son. The fantasy of the infanticide appears as the answer to an unbearable pain turning into its very opposite.

This is how Millie's final reaction should be read. Her meeting with the young murderer, who is as helpless as a child and whose voice is 'the little voice of a child talking in his sleep' (p. 136), summons up an unknown maternal flutter in her heart, the very flower of sterility:

> A strange dreadful feeling gripped Millie Evans' bosom — some seed that had never flourished there, unfolded, and struck deep roots and burst into painful leaf. (p. 136)

Such a feeling unveils an unendurable wound that is to be cauterized; her inner turmoil then suddenly transforms her gentleness towards the young man into its reverse, i.e., a loathsome cry sentencing him to death, as if she was killing the infant that had just blossomed in her bosom. 'Go it! Go it! A — ah, Sid! Shoot 'im down. Shoot 'im!' (p. 137), she says plunging with these words into the murderous world of men.

The child in 'The Woman at the Store' is also trapped by a double bind. On the one hand, she is the living repository of a deadly secret — the murder of her father by her mother — which is locked up in her as a picture she will eventually draw. On the other hand, her mother threatens to kill her if she lets out the secret. It seems there is no way out from death but death, and once more the fantasy of the infanticide comes up to smother suffering, this time the child's, directed against herself and mirroring the collapse of the woman's identity caused by loneliness and impending madness. The story is caught in a vicious circle where violence is all pervasive and where there are no words to soothe pain since only the nothingness of loneliness can answer the despair of death.

Such a grim view of things raises questions, and one can wonder if openings can be found and if suffering eventually loses its edge to open up to a psychic space where it can be alleviated through mourning and the loss accepted as such.

Death is often connected with closed-up places, as for instance Miss Brill's tomb-like box, or the little girl's inner self shut up on her secret, etc. Actually Miss Brill's ultimate gesture when burying her last cry in a box refers to her psychic death, for nothing more of her sorrow will ever be expressed afterwards. She is in a way buried alive just as Ma Parker is in her desperate quest for a place where she could let her tears flow out. Wanderings lead nowhere. There is no way out of the dilemma. On the one hand, there is no place to cry, as if there was no inner space for it, and, on the other hand, the craving for tears stands for interment too: 'if at last, after all these years, she were to cry, she'd find herself in the lock-up as like as not' (p. 407). There is no way of releasing sorrow, as is suggested by the first words of 'The Child-Who-Was-Tired': 'a little road that led nowhere'. This tearless woe is enclosed in what we could call a tomb-like bosom, Ma's or that of the canary's owner. I think the lack of a psychic space to mourn has the effect of fetishizing the dead love-object because its loss cannot be inscribed anywhere.

This is exactly how Laura feels about the garden party: 'kisses, voices, tinkling spoons, laughter, the smell of crushed grass were somehow inside her. She had no room for anything else' (p. 497). In 'The Garden Party' too mourning is cancelled out, and must consequently be read differently from the commonly received interpretations. No doubt Laura goes through a new vision of life, for she is faced with suffering and poverty for the first time, but she misses the last step in her experience and fails to understand what death actually means.

She travels inwardly but cannot get beyond the halfway mark. Surprisingly enough, when she is in front of the deceased young man, the outward signs of gloom and mourning fade out; so does the signifier 'dead' which is replaced by an opposite series of signifiers such as 'sleep', 'dreaming', 'wonderful', 'beautiful', 'marvel' and 'marvellous' (pp. 498-499). The young man, like the Sleeping Beauty, strikes her as an image of suspended death, as if he could be awakened by a caress — an impression which is hinted at even though it is denied: 'never wake him up again' (p. 498). These words appear to me as highly connotated and give me the impression that something was going astray, as though the road taken by Laura could not lead her where she was bound for, but elsewhere, to a marvellous world, Fenella's world, for example — a space completely out of step with actual death and with the feeling of horror and void it should convey. Upon seeing the deceased young man — 'look[ing] a picture' (p. 498), says the text — Laura is at once carried away into a 'marvellous' world as if, at the very moment of reaching the other gloomy shore, she transformed it into its opposite: life itself. 'Isn't life...' (p. 499), she sobs. She does not finish her sentence just as she does not complete her experience; from the dialectic life and death coupling, she retains only life. She cannot utter the word 'death'; since it is not the turning point of her experience, it has no reality for her.

Indeed the gap created by death is filled up with the completeness of the pair Laurie and Laura, for their names represent the two halves of a perfect entity where loss is not taken into account: this is clearly illustrated by the sudden apparition of Laurie, who is the other young man's substitute, thus negating any vacant space.

In this perspective, Katherine Mansfield's story becomes even more subtle, for it shows the incomplete experience of a young girl who, because she is too young and not really involved in the situation, thinks she has seen all and understood all — including death — whereas she has only just started to move out of her protected social and family circle.

Disruptions in the text of Katherine Mansfield's stories thus point to the vacant space of impossible mourning, to the silent words of unexpressed grief. In these disruptions the voice of Katherine Mansfield as a woman can be heard under the voice of the artist. Yet the artist is there and transcends the despair in the life/death dialectic through her artistic creation, i.e., by interweaving the two strands and thus giving life to what has already disappeared: 'We can see death in life as we can see death in a flower that is fresh unfolded — our hymn is to the flower's beauty.'[4] Indeed the canary's 'joyful little singing' remains alive beyond nothingness, or, in 'The Voyage', while the 'text' inscribes in its big black frame the vanishing of a blissful world '*Lost!* . . . GONE FOR EVER!' (p. 476), the process of writing simultaneously recreates that world of marvel. Other images take us further in the intensity of grief and in its artistic resolution. The glimpse of agony captured in the martyred child's awful drawing can be seen as a first bleeding movement towards artistic expression. Towards the ink with which the artist's writing gesture is transcribed. The 'boss' who is incapable of weeping because he is caught up in a sterile and wilful intention — 'he intended, he had arranged to weep . . .' (p. 531) — sheds ink-tears in which he drowns the fly in order to drown the father's memory in ink as the only means of reaching the other shore. This is how Katherine Mansfield writes: she drowns death into oblivion[5] with her ink, but she also writes out its abyss of yawning nothingness and sublimates it by conjuring her readers elsewhere, by taking us, our backs turned to gloom and sadness, into the magic world of childhood.

NOTES

1. This is what Kate Fullbrook suggests in *Katherine Mansfield* (Brighton: The Harvester Press, 1987).

2. See Clare Hanson and Andrew Gurr, *Katherine Mansfield* (New York: St. Martin's Press, 1981): 'we are all ultimately solitary, and human beings are fundamentally cruel and indifferent to one another except in the rare instances where they love' (p. 81). I support this view of Miss Brill although I would like to stress Katherine Mansfield's implicit philosophical approach, which becomes obvious when one realizes that such pervasive themes amount to concepts.

3. See Serge Leclaire's concept of the 'marvellous' in *On tue un enfant* (Paris: Seuil, 1975).

4. Katherine Mansfield, *Letters and Journals*, edited by C.K. Stead (Harmondsworth: Penguin, 1977), p. 135.

5. In this respect, one should closely examine biographical elements — as I intend to do in the book I am writing on Katherine Mansfield — for this will show that Katherine Mansfield's death trauma pattern is first and foremost connected with the death of her little sister Gwen, Chummie's death being only the reiteration of the first trauma.

Fauna and Flora in Katherine Mansfield's Short Stories

FRANCINE TOLRON

D.M. Davin considers that some of the obvious features of Katherine Mansfield's style are:

> a sensibility almost morbidly alert to detail and to the evidence of the senses, to colour and shape, to the feel, smell and sound of things . . . an exultation in life, movement and beauty and an appalled shrinking before the crude, the ugly and the cruel.[1]

Her great sensuousness and keen sensitiveness are reflected in her treatment of the various plants and animals which appear in her stories: they are transient but recurrent images whose sum makes up a coherent pattern which exemplifies both her 'exultation in life' and her 'shrinking before the crude'.

Nature appears in her stories as both positive and negative; the plant and animal images are never mere 'decorative' elements, they are meant to express the protagonists' psyche, their transient moods or states of being, their response to life or to a particularly vital moment.

In 'Prelude' nature is shown as simple, carnal, domestic, as a source of joy and beneficial effects, as exemplified by the tasty jams Linda's mother intends to make. More significantly, the first attitude of Katherine Mansfield's heroes — and heroines above all — is to perceive nature as an object of admiration: it is perfect in its form and colours and thus transcends the daily humdrum. It provides a short-lived ecstasy. One thinks of Bertha, in 'Bliss', and of the rapture which takes hold of her when she gazes at the lovely fruit on the table or at the pear tree, a true miracle of perfection. Similarly, Linda Burnell goes into ecstasy over the exquisite flowers of the manuka tree. Flowers and fruit are combined to materialize the feeling of plenitude which overcomes the characters. Leila, in 'Her First Ball', caught in the whirling motion of the dance, feels 'like a flower that is tossed into a pool' (p. 429); meanwhile the young men are getting ready for the ritual of seduction, like birds strutting before the love dance, 'smoothing their gloves, patting their glossy hair'

(p. 428). The attachment that links the young couple in 'Psychology' calls for a blossoming into a physical intercourse, as suggested by the author's very words: 'now was the time for harvest — harvest' (p. 319). In this respect, 'Feuille d'Album' is delightfully explicit: the nascent love of the artist for the unknown girl he is observing materializes into flowers and his heart literally becomes the daffodils she is presently watering. The egg he gives her is the naïve, preposterous manifestation of his youthful passion. Significantly, the whole scene takes place on a background made of spring rain, of fragances of wet earth, of budding trees: it is both cosmic and humble, touching and slightly puerile — like love shared by two young people. But one must not be deceived by the seemingly gleeful, rosy-coloured atmosphere: the satirical Katherine Mansfield, whose verve can be so acid, cannot miss out the opportunity of denouncing the mawkishness of some of her characters. Nature is sometimes linked to affectation as, for instance, in 'The Garden Party' where José is presented as a butterfly in 'silk petticoat' and 'kimono jacket', while the bushes bow down 'as though they had been visited by archangels'. The enamoured Henry, in 'Something Childish But Very Natural', sees his dream-cottage walk 'on tiptoe'.

Personified and animated by a cheap imagination these elements become part of the characters' simple, childish psyche and mean yearnings. The tone becomes distressing in 'Miss Brill' when the elderly spinster marvels at seeing, through her reductive vision, that the surrounding world is a stage and that the little dog by her side 'trotted off, like a little "theatre" dog' (p. 376). This must be interpreted as a means of depicting derision in human life.

Apart from these few, almost comical examples, the prevailing trend in her stories is to glorify the animal and the vegetal world. Plenitude and bliss shine out in 'Marriage à la Mode' where the sorrow William feels for his lost conjugal happiness is emblematically and a *contrario* expressed by the image of the rose-bush:

> When he had been a little boy, it was his delight to run into the garden after a shower of rain and shake the rose-bush over him. Isabel was that rose-bush, petal-soft, sparkling and cool. (p. 433)

In a less striking way, dead love is conjured up in 'A Dill Pickle', by a profusion of geranium, marigold and verbena, bathed in warm sunshine. In 'Something Childish But Very Natural' the beloved Edna with her 'marigold hair' and 'strawberry cheeks' is a flower-woman and a fruit-woman; at the beginning of the story, the eponymous poem heralds the sentimental fervour which is to take hold of Henry by referring to the flying bird heading for his beloved.

Nature is resolutely endowed with life and a momentum which, at first, remain untouched. Henry, again, who works for a London architect, dreams of building nests, not houses. When the highly perturbed Edna refuses to yield to him, he evades his vexation and grief by gazing at the trees of the square 'with their unbroken buds'. A similar reaction is to be found in 'Psychology'; the young woman has been deserted by her friend and is a prey to the adoration of the 'elderly virgin' with the posy:

> for a moment she did not take the violets ... Again she saw ... the dark garden ringed with glittering ivy, the willows ... she put her arms round her friend. (p. 323)

And she accepts her violets, shrivelled as they may be. Nature provides an answer to an unsatisfied expectation, a transitory evasion, a brief liberation. In 'At the Bay' Beryl changes into a turtle and a rat to have a swim and escape from Mrs Harry Kember. Through such a metamorphosis, she means to protect herself and get away from the 'poisoning', pernicious influence of 'this cold woman' whom yet 'she longed to hear'. She shuts herself up in the hermetic shell of a turtle or the swift repulsive appearance of the fleeing rat, very much in the same manner as a child at play pretends to believe that a hiding-place is a real shelter. The turtle and the rat, significantly both marine elements (as stated by the text), are synonymous with transitory safeness, away from the dangers of dry land (the blemish of adulthood?). In 'Her First Ball', Leila eludes the hold of the old beau and of his ill-omened talk by thinking of the pleasant comfort of home:

> She wanted to be home, or sitting on the verandah listening to those baby owls. (p. 431)

Similarly, in 'Life of Ma Parker', the old drudge, overwhelmed with grief, puts an end to her misfortunes by flying toward oblivion and death: 'the icy wind blew out her apron into a balloon' (p. 408).

A negative aspect of nature is becoming apparent, i.e., nature as refuge, as ersatz, deprived of its joy, disquieting. It is even presented as heavy with dangers. The beginning of 'At the Bay' suggests an engulfment by an almost diluvian tidal wave: 'it looked as though ...

one immense wave had come rippling, rippling — how far?' (p. 441); and it is made more threatening by the apparition of the huge fish at the window. This childhood phantasmagoria, taken up throughout the story, together with the animal and vegetal imagery helps generate a feeling of uneasiness, some vague anguish powerfully shared by the characters and the reader. The threat begins to take shape with the allusion to a 'sea-forest', a sort of Gordian knot made of seaweeds and of 'thread-like creatures' where submarine sheep are heard bleating: some antipodean Lorelei and Atlantis? It may be so: in any case fauna and flora are suggestive of death; some devouring, suckling – down process is hinted at against which the characters are utterly powerless. Nature holds man under its spell.

The garden, in 'At the Bay', that Jonathan describes as 'vast, dangerous . . . undiscovered, unexplored', speaks and entices the frustrated Beryl into consuming sexual intercourse with the not very commendable Harry: 'How had she got here? The stern garden asked her as the gate pushed open, and quick as a cat Harry Kembler came through and snatched her to him' (p. 469). Beryl's disgusted exclamation: 'You are vile, vile' condenses the horror that human baseness and nature's conniving deceitfulness fill her with. Similarly, in 'Prelude', another scene, bringing together in an (imaginary?) relation Beryl and a young man in a (primeval?) garden, is bathed in a similar atmosphere of shady temptation: he is described as 'sly and laughing' and she turns him away by dressing herself. Does this mean that sexual intercourse is demeaning? Not quite, but it is referred to as difficult, impossible and bringing little gratification. These scenes take place in the night, with which the moon, cold and morbid, is associated. The phallic pear tree in 'Bliss' is bathed in the white moonlight and the lunar Miss Fulton, turns out to be a femme fatale. In 'Prelude' Linda turns away her husband's overtures as she finds herself shivering in the midst of 'a flood of cold light' (p. 243).

A fundamental aspect of Katherine Mansfield's universe is thus revealed, namely an overwhelming sense of waste. This is a recurrent theme in her short stories. Henry, as he is waiting for Edna, mistakes for a moth the little girl who is bringing the message whose reading will fill the garden and cottage with shadows, spinning 'a web of darkness' around him. Laura leaves the garden party with the sensation of grass crushed by the guests' feet. William, the deserted husband, calls his existence 'a filthy life' and his dejection finds a powerful metaphorical expression in the landscape he is gazing at: 'One bird drifted high like a dark fleck in a jewel'. We are here poles apart from the ecstasy of 'Bliss'.

Animals and plants are sometimes used as 'objective correlatives' to this world-weariness. The flower of the manuka-tree soon loses its petals which get caught in Linda's hair: from an 'exquisite small thing', it turns into 'a horrid little thing'. Now, 'horrid' implies an intention, somewhere, around which the mystery remains entire: 'Why, then, flower at all?' is the only appropriate answer, an interrogation about life whether human, animal or vegetal... There remains only to lament, along with Linda, over 'all these things that are wasted, wasted.... It was uncanny' (p. 452).

Man's powerlessness is also matched by the reflection it finds in nature: in 'Prelude', the aloe is cruel, in 'The Canary', the bird dies for all the devoted love of its mistress who deplores:

> I must confess that there does seem to me something sad in life ... It is there, deep down, deep down, part of one, like one's breathing. (p. 541)

Such bitterness is echoed in the questions punctuating 'At the Bay': 'What was going on down there?', 'Was there no escape?' asks Linda, feeling like a leaf that is shaken by the wind; 'the shortness of life' exclaims Jonathan, insect-like, prisoner of his own life. Through the imagery Katherine Mansfield conveys what words cannot express, i.e., a pure metaphysical anguish.

Yet, she also uses animal images to express occasional healthy outbursts of hatred against social injustice, which roots her work in the concrete. In 'The Doll's House', the washerwoman's poor daughters are 'shooed out like chickens'. Alice, the young maid in 'Prelude', is compared to the hapless duck victimized by the children:

> It was hard to say which of the two, Alice or the duck, looked the better basted ... they both had the same air of gloss and strain. (p. 251)

As shown in these two quotations, Katherine Mansfield uses animal metaphors when she ventures into the field of social criticism, but also... in her rendering of married life. In 'Prelude', Linda sees her husband as 'a frog', 'a big fat turkey' or a good cumbersome dog:

> If only he wouldn't jump at her so, and bark so loudly, and watch her with such eager, loving eyes. (p. 254)

Childhood and art are not spared either by her scathing pen: the children in 'Prelude' desert their improvised doll's tea party, consisting in flowers and greenery which will be eaten up by ants and snails. As to the artist, in 'Feuille d'Album', what he sees in the market below — a source of inspiration to him, one might think — is a swarming world of crab-like costermongers — 'among the flowers the old women scuttled from side to side, like crabs' (p. 268) — on whom he spits his prune-stones...

'Sun and Moon' is very significant in that the short span of time it covers and the thinness of the argument (a party given at some wealthy people's, seen through their two children's eyes) heighten the value and meaning of each tiny detail. The description of the scene, both before and after the meal, and of the children is interspersed with references, comparisons and allusions to animals and plants which clearly bring out the two basic functions of Katherine Mansfield's use of nature images: 'an exultation in life, movement, and beauty and an appalled shrinking before the crude, the ugly and the cruel'. On the set table, 'the salt-cellars were tiny birds drinking out of basins', 'in the middle was a lake with rose petals floating on it', the napkins are 'made into roses', in the lit-up dining-room 'all the lights were red roses'; Sun, the little boy, is dolled up in 'a white shirt with red and white daisies speckled on it', male-guests in tailcoats look funnily 'like beetles' and the children's apparition, all dressed-up, causes the company to exclaim: 'my lamb' (Nurse), 'oh, the ducks! Oh, the lambs!' (the ladies), before their mother tells them to 'fly up to [their] little nest'. But the glee will be short-lived. Among the guests, Sun singles out one man to whom he takes an instant liking. The man asks Sun if he is fond of dogs, then vanishes. Sun 'thought perhaps he'd gone outside to fetch in a puppy'... but nothing comes out of the brief encounter. The only episode standing out against the ambient artificiality leads nowhere: no real dog will ever materialize. When later in the night the two children wake up, the party is drawing to an end and the atmosphere is heavy with inebriated mirth: Sun is horrified to see the shattered beauty of the table (ribbons and roses pulled untied, 'bones and bits and fruit peels and shells everywhere' (p. 304), whereas Moon, undisturbed, bites into the nut, the only remnant of the ice pudding which had been made to look like a little pink house, with white snow on the roof, green windows and a brown door where the nut served as a handle. To Sun, the broken little house is a heart-breaking sight; to Moon it is immaterial. Significantly, as early as the fifth line of the story, our attention had been drawn to a difference in the two children's perception. While watching the men carrying the flower pots for the reception, Moon said 'Look. There's a man wearing a palm on his head' (p. 300) and her remark is followed by 'But she never knew the difference between real things and not real ones'. As in 'Sun and Moon', much of Katherine Mansfield's writings deal with growing up i.e., the difficulty of coming to terms with reality, and with the power of imagination to transcend it.

I hope I have shown that there exists in Katherine Mansfield's stories a real bestiary, a proper Mansfieldian nature which deserves to be fully explored. The meaning of her nature imagery is as complex as that of her stories: each element in it stands both for one thing and its opposite according to how the author's perception evolves from one story to another or even within a single story. Whether used as mere narrative element integrated into the plot, or used metaphorically or metonymically, the fauna and flora references weave an almost ecological pattern which reflects a social and/or psychological reality, and eventually Katherine Mansfield's fundamental questioning about life — an ecological pattern that attracts or rejects, bewitches or repels her characters and thus forcefully and pitilessly defines the human condition.

NOTES

1. D. M. Davin, introduction to: Katherine Mansfield, *Selected Stories* (Oxford: Oxford University Press, 1953), p. xv.

FROM READING TO WRITING

Point Counterpoint:
Both Sides of the Broad Road in Katherine Mansfield's 'The Garden Party' and Witi Ihimaera's 'This Life is Weary'

CAROLE FROUDE DURIX

In 1989 Penguin is publishing *Dear Miss Mansfield*,[1] a collection of short stories by Witi Ihimaera to commemorate the centenary of her birth. The book begins with a letter from the author to Miss Mansfield which sets the context; it is followed by a novella-length story entitled 'Maata' which was inspired by the relationship between Katherine Mansfield and her school friend, Maata Mahupuku. A series of short stories follows that are either variations on, or inspired by, Katherine Mansfield's stories: 'The Woman at the Store', 'How Pearl Button Was Kidnapped', 'The Doll's House', 'Prelude', 'Her First Ball', 'Something Childish But Very Natural', 'At the Bay' and 'The Garden Party'. Ihimaera states that his aim was not to imitate or mimic Katherine Mansfield but rather to respond to her. To do this he has written stories which are variations linked at differing levels to the Mansfield original.

'This Life is Weary', one of these seventeen stories, is to be read in parallel to 'The Garden Party', written by Katherine Mansfield in 1921. Ihimaera states in his introduction:

> 'The Garden Party' is one of Katherine Mansfield's most respected and finely constructed stories, counterpointing Laura's feeling about the garden party itself with the news that a young man [Scott], from one of the cottages 'down below', has that very day been killed.

Ihimaera presents his version of the day's events through the eyes of the dead man's children. His narration however is untainted by the tragedy since throughout the day the young spectators are quite unaware of their father's accident.

***

Katherine Mansfield's house, Tinakori Road, Wellington

The geographical dichotomy of the two stories is materialized by the broad road that runs between the big house up above and the cottages 'down below'; this separation affects the attitudes of both the authors and the characters in these stories. If the general setting remains identical the focalization varies greatly because of the very different angles of approach. The Mansfield story views the events from the Big House whereas 'This Life is Weary' is firmly established 'down below'. A comparison of the sequencing of events in the two stories immediately confronts the demands of the two very different departure points. If the Mansfield text immediately involves the reader in the 'action' of the preparations for the garden party by the retrospective jump into the recent past — 'And after all' —, Ihimaera has chosen to place the narrator outside the text by introducing the background of the children through whose eyes the reader is to view the festivities at 'the Big House'.

Katherine Mansfield introduces us to a picture close to paradise when even the weather and the blooming of the roses seem to fall under the control of the Sheridans; in the space of one night each bush has produced an innumerable quantity of blooms which will help to duly impress the carefully selected guests at the garden party. This illusory but apparent control of the uncontrollable by the hosts serves to underline the importance of the façade that high society wishes to present to their own world of acquaintances and their innate blindness to the true reality of their way of life.

The unfortunate 'incident' of the tragic accident brings the existence of the poor miserable cottages 'down below' to the unwilling notice of the Sheridan family just before the garden party; Mansfield's description of the location eloquently illustrates the Sheridans' distaste at being confronted not only with an event that disturbs their sheltered way of life but also their ability to close their eyes to the existence of people outside their class. If Laura's uneasy conscience objects to the garden party 'with a man dead just outside the front gate', the narrator rectifies the assertion by distancing the cottages 'in a lane to themselves at the very bottom of a steep rise that led up to the house. A broad road ran between'. The cottages appear more remote, isolated in the lower reaches of a valley, which is in keeping with the lowly rank of their inhabitants; yet if these mean dwellings mar the countryside the presence of their occupants in the service of the Sheridans and their like is accepted as quite normal. In contrast, the Scott children's experience vis-à-vis the Big House is regarded as a game in which Ihimaera even takes up the 'oh so lovely' turn of phrase of the Mansfield story. Here too the broad road runs between the two worlds. The world of fantasy of the children is accepted by the adult world of 'down below'. In this society, a belief in down-to-earth good sense and the equality of all men is one of the main principles of daily life even if hardship is at times alleviated by dreams.

Ihimaera opens his story by a factual description of the cottages in which he uses the terms that Katherine Mansfield evolved in the second part of her story. This displacement of text presents the cottages as a protected earthly environment where the happiness of the inhabitants is based on the stern reality of life rather than on the superficial façades raised to impress the outside world. Seen from the Big House these dwellings are mean and are painted a dingy chocolate brown; they are deprived — the gardens are mere 'patches' which house 'sick hens' and produce only 'cabbage stalks'. In contrast, Ihimaera's John Scott lives in 'the land of chocolate brown houses' — a phrase that evokes fairytale houses in a land of plenty, the plenitude of which is defined in terms of love and relationship rather than materialistic outward show. In the original text, the smoke coming out of the cottage chimney 'was poverty-stricken' and described in terms of rags and shreds, which underlines the Sheridans' overlying vision of the poor. Ihimaera modulates this 'was' to 'might be', thus inserting an element of uncertainty in the terms and implying perhaps that true richness can be defined otherwise and lies elsewhere. Both texts refer to the 'great silvery plumes that uncurled' from the Big House chimneys but, whereas in the original story the phrase evokes the grandeur of [ostrich] feathers that are a possible decoration in a garden party, Ihimaera reverts to the natural world by alluding to the fact that the presence of John Scott is inevitably accompanied by the singing of larks.

The social awareness of the two communities is defined by both authors but the emphasis varies greatly. In 'The Garden Party' the superior social position of the Sheridans is an accepted fact — signs of financial prosperity are to be found everywhere: canna lilies in profusion, new hats, cream buns from Godber's and the grand marquee for the party. The reader gradually becomes aware of the futility of the social proprieties which are given such importance — the emptiness of Laura's telephone conversation, the hollowness of the contacts formed during the mundane afternoon, Mrs Sheridan's complete insensitivity to human relationships and emotions. Mrs

Sheridan *knows* that the dead man's family wouldn't expect them to cancel their party, she scolds Laura for putting a cloud over their joyous expectations for the coming afternoon; after the party she inwardly reproaches her husband for bringing up the subject again, thus spoiling the retrospective pleasure. Finally, she reacts by filling up a charitable basket of their left-overs (suddenly deemed 'perfectly good food') which Laura is to give to the bereaved family so that they can be one up on their neighbours even in this time of sadness. This shows her complete ignorance of the concerns of the people 'down below'. Laura, despite her youth, is the only character who appears to be able to conceive of another circle than her own; although she endeavours to fit in with the social niceties of her class she constantly displays a certain malaise: indeed when she gives the workmen directives for the setting up of the marquee she tries to imitate her mother's manner but immediately realizes how artificial this façade is; yet when she tries to be natural and eats her bread and butter she feels uncomfortable. She is attracted to the friendliness and her own romanticized picture of the genuine relationships in the working class but she cannot escape across the broad road that separates her from them.

Both Mrs Sheridan and Mrs Scott agree about the 'swarming' children 'down below': the former does not wish her family to mix and the latter firmly sends the children to school during the week and thinks that at the weekend her little ones are better observing the Big House with their subsequent creative activities as they note, draw and judge what they have carefully observed. Indeed, their observations display a definite accuracy of judgement and, while their deference for the upper classes which are 'seen from afar' is manifest, it does not modify the opinion that the musicality of Meg and José leaves much to be desired or that certain beaux could not possibly pretend to gain the affection or respect of the girls. Even when Dadda jokingly comments that 'Some of what they see might rub off on them' the overall idea in the writing is that improvement will be achieved by hard work and a sound education rather than trying to climb the social ladder. The initial values on which the life style of the two communities are based are radically different.

Ihimaera insists on the closeness to nature of the cottage community; Jack Scott is popular with everybody but mutual respect reigns, for the women may tease and admire but they know that he will always be loyal to Em. Moreover he appears as a D.H. Lawrence-like character when his earthiness is disclosed — his love for Em is manifest and the children that are the fruit of their marriage are considered as gifts of God. Although Em has lost what beauty she had because of repeated child-bearing, she continues to consider her body and the pleasure it can give as a worthy gift for her spouse. Yet this respect for the physical which highlights the value attributed to the façade in the Mansfield story is counterbalanced by the inner wealth of character; even the children could appreciate the depth of respect that Jack Scott felt for his wife:

> Despite the poverty of their situation, Mam was a lady — as much a lady as any up at The Big House. This did not mean that Mam had airs, oh no. What it meant was that her manner was decorous and her manners and modesty becoming to her in her husband's eyes.

The Mansfield story devotes comparatively little space to the actual garden party and concentrates on the preparations for it and on Laura's subsequent visit to the cottage; Ihimaera prolongs and broadens the garden party by amply quoting from the original narration and then doubling this up with the Scott children's day. In this way the quotations are respected except that the 'you' is now applied to 'the children'. The text is enriched, for, while the Mansfield story informs us essentially of the family's preparations, Ihimaera broadens the outlook: in 'The Garden Party' we are told that the gardener has been up since dawn and we admire the finished result of his work whereas in 'This Life is Weary', we witness the cutting of the lawn in minute detail. Celia informs us that it is going to be a beautiful day, which lengthens the time within the narration to correspond to the length of a working day. The Ihimaera story adds focus to the party by placing it in parallel with the children's own garden party in the shadows beneath the trees. Their dancing is accompanied by the same band whose tuba player draws them further into the festivities by sending one of the waiters to serve them cakes and cream puffs.

Ihimaera further lengthens the 'time' of the garden party, for each incident is re-enacted by the children's written or drawn account — the event is an excuse for communication and self-expression; the party enables the children to escape from their little world into another social circle and another world of imagination and creativity whereas the reaction of the Sheridan household is completely different. All the guests are ready to agree that the party was a great success but the surface enjoyment is betrayed by the obvious let-down once all the guests have left; the Sheridans go into the empty marquee, Mrs Sheridan is exhausted, and the formal enjoyment so recently appreciated has completely disappeared; the garden party is depicted as a mere incident in their lives. Ihimaera clearly plays these two attitudes against one another, for if Katherine Mansfield *shows* the reader the superficiality of the garden party, Ihimaera produces it as a scene that reflects life as a stage. He consciously uses his authorial control in his description of the theatre where the garden party takes place. At the beginning of his story Ihimaera establishes the departure point and modifies Katherine Mansfield's vision of the cottages so that they do not appear as a 'dark, dirty eyesore'. The reader's knowledge of their decrepit presence, however, enhances the contrast when he introduces the children's version of the festivities. From the start Laura assumes the role of stage director governing the setting. In parallel, Celia describes the light blue and gold backdrop surrounding the residence that resembles a two-storied doll's house such as those represented on chocolate boxes. By using this comparison Ihimaera emphasizes the marvellous aspect of high-society circles for the children — chocolate boxes are for the eyes and contain the promise of the wonders within. The children taste such delights but only rarely so that the anticipation is all the greater. Similarly the Scott children spend the week preceding the party conjecturing about the wonderful 'performance' they are going to observe. It is as if they have 'paid 3d to cheer up a drab afternoon'. The different areas of the 'stage' are brought into focus, successively highlighting the various actors: the band in the foreground that constitutes a bridge between the children and the 'actors', the perfectly-mown grass where the guests seem to glide into different formations, the balcony where the family move up or down stage. Whereas Katherine Mansfield underlines the gracious moving of the guests into varying groups that are endemic in the social etiquette of such occasions, Ihimaera consciously underlines the roles that are acted for the benefit of social position, and thus, the underlying lack of sincerity of the Mansfield characters informs his narration and pinpoints the *aroha* present in the relationships of the people 'down below'.

In both stories, Laura is central, for she is the essential link between the two communities; she is aware of the divide although too young to be able to define the phenomenon. She is the heroine for the 'star-struck audience' and there is an obvious identification between Laura and Celia; when Laura entertains her dolls for tea on the tennis court she has moved downstage from the house towards the children; her guests include a 'princess Celia', a title that Thomas adopts for his sister when inviting her to dance during their 'garden party' under the trees. There is a certain interchange of traits, for, although Laura belongs to a kind of dream world of 'fascinating golden creatures', she also fantasizes on the genuineness of the conversation with the workmen, wonders at the sensibility of the one who enjoys the perfume of the lavenders and judges them far more interesting than the silly young men that she has to frequent. Conversely Thomas, 'the most accurate observer of them all', perceives in the 'perfect little princess' a streak of the tomboy and a lack of feminity in the cartwheels she performs across the lawn or in the thumbing of her nose at Meg's beaux! Or again, while Em recognizes the signs that Celia is becoming a woman, Mrs Sheridan hails Laura's maturity by bestowing the adorable little hat, the symbol of the feminine façade that a woman must give society. Down below, Dadda loves Em because she is a true lady of modesty whereas Mrs Sheridan represents a world of pretence as she fans herself *like* a lady in her upstairs window; the picture of grandeur is cruelly deflated in the Ihimaera story when the scene is recreated on paper rather like a cartoon with the caption that Mrs Sheridan is trying to swat at something going 'Bzz bzz bzz'!

In both stories a mirror reflects the surrounding world: in Katherine Mansfield, Mrs Sheridan pops the hat on Laura's head just at the moment when Laura not only brings disturbing news but also expresses an attitude that does not fit the behaviour of her class. Her mother tries to change the subject of their conversation by flattering her daughter's pride in her appearance. She says: '"I have never seen you look such a picture. Look at yourself!" And she held up her hand-mirror' (p. 495). The outward façade is there to blind these people to the hard realities of life that may disturb their comfort. Their world turns constantly inward, the perfect mirror reflects the image of the self and its protected environment; it excludes reality. Interestingly enough, Laura rejects her mother's reasoning for an instant when she abruptly leaves the room, but the moment she enters her own domain she is confronted and seduced by her own reflection; the ambivalence of her instant of internal conflict becomes more remote; her unease is calmed by the reassuring image that she perceives of herself and her place in her community. Although the reflection she observes is at first impersonal and separate from her own being, it is sufficient to overcome her doubts about her behaviour so that when she thinks of the dead man and imagines his return home 'it all seem[s] blurred, unreal, like a picture in the newspaper' (p. 495). The image is put to one side and momentarily falls into the accepted perspective of the family.

The reflection that Em perceives is quite different: at the outset her mirror is 'cracked' and 'stained' and so incapable of projecting a perfect picture. The mirror, far from reassuring the perceiver, confirms the ravages that time and this weary life have wrought; ageing is evident — Em's skin has coarsened and her red hair greyed. The mirror reflects the physical truth but this reality is amply compensated by the fundamental verity of human relationships and love.

Jack Scott's philosophy informs the overall discussion of death supplied by the two stories and their very different final visions. Both use the garden party to counterpoint the reactions to the fatal accident. Laura is the central catalyzer in Mansfield's story and the author tries to illustrate that, in contrast to her family, the workman's death contributes to her personal development because she involves herself in the tragedy. It is dusk as she closes their garden gates; in so doing she temporarily breaks with her own environment and her own way of life since her visit is not wholly approved of at home. Indeed, the fact that her mother decides not to express her fears and apprehension about Laura's action is significant. Laura's descent to the cottages is synonymous with a descent into the netherworld; it is heralded by the passage of a big dog — could this be Cerberus who guards Hades? Little by little the reader becomes aware of the contrast between this somber shadowy world and the elements of brightness and lightness included in the description of Laura who still remains in the atmosphere of the garden party; she cannot initially integrate the reality of her mission because her mind goes over the recent party and 'she ha[s] no room for anything else'. Katherine Mansfield concretizes the divide with the crossing of the broad road; gradually the initiatory descent becomes the end of a dream and the ultimate revelation of new values. The brightness and gaiety of the afternoon are replaced by smoke and darkness, the glittering dresses give way to shawls and tweed caps, a low hum is substituted to the voices and tinkling spoons, her own attire, so admired above the broad road becomes so totally unsuitable that Laura hesitates but is irresistibly drawn on, the inhabitants of the cottage driving her forward. To her question 'Are you Mrs Scott?' she is told to walk in; no matter how hard Laura tries to control and cut short the visit, she has to submit to the sequence of events that are pre-destined. When she is finally confronted with the dead man on his bed, the rhythm of the narration is completely transformed; the pace slows down, the tone becomes tranquil. Laura at last finds peace with her confused feelings; the reality of dreadful death is reconciled with this somewhat romanticized vision of the dead man. He is the incarnation of the philosophy that was his when he was alive, namely that all are equal in the face of God and in death; he represents the dream, the perfect, the impossible in life. 'His eyes were closed; they were blind under the closed eyelids.' The implication is that this wonderful representation of death is beyond all those things that Laura and her family deem important. Yet, in spite of this revelation, Laura is not quite freed of her pre-conceived ideas, for, although the image is perfect, she feels she *has* to cry and she *cannot* go out of the room without a word. Her attitude is ambivalent and vacillates between her need to comprehend and her education which provides a given reaction to a set occasion; although she begs forgiveness for the hat, the symbol of her growing up and of her class, she reverts in some ways to the superficial, mundane social formulas of her society, which confirms her comparative lack of involvement in the tragedy. In spite of this duality the encounter is the turning point in her initiation to adulthood for she can immediately control the situation: these people no longer drive her along paths which she is hesitant to take, she finds her own way out of the house and away from the dark people. When she meets Laurie the reader realizes that her attitude to relationship has matured: if before the party she impulsively gives Laurie a small quick squeeze, now she takes his arm and presses up to him. She has had a glimpse of the afterlife which has given her a concept of duration and time outside the timeless frivolities of society circles. However, she remains unable to articulate this experience, which perhaps indicates that it is not wholly conclusive. Her encounter with death is romanticized but remains unassimilated; doubtlessly this is because the dead man is unknown to her and so she feels little emotional loss.

In the Ihimaera story Laura's educating experience is eclipsed. When finally the children decide to walk home the description of the descent to the cottages is considerably condensed compared to the Mansfield story; the sordidness of the place is mentioned; in the darkness the people are likened to wraiths, synonymous with death, but the focus is on the two young people whom they come across but do not recognize because of the darkness. Then comes the excited rush home to tell of the day's doings. Celia alone is aware of 'an awful aching feeling' in her heart. This sensation is to be placed side by side with the moment when the man from Godber's is talking to the cook. Ihimaera ends his sentence with 'and —' omitting the Mansfield information and yet alluding to it so that the reader who is familiar with 'The Garden Party' can complete the story. The ellipsis, in the same way as Mrs Sheridan's ellipsis in the original story when Laura sets out for the cottage, renders the ensuing events all the more telling. In the following paragraph, Ihimaera indirectly alludes to Dadda's death:

> Suddenly the sky was filled with a soft radiance and it was going almost like — like a shooting star, in the daytime, going up into the sky — and Celia felt such sweet pain that she wanted to weep. Her heart was so full, so overflowing, so brimming over, and in that instant she thought of her Dadda.

The light that has been dancing on the guests of the Big House seems suddenly concentrated in the sky; the language takes on the biblical resonances of the ascension: the 'soft radiance' contrasts with the momentary shooting star, a term immediately contradicted by the time of day. This unarticulated, transcendental image of death and resurrection emotionally overwhelms Celia and yet she is unaware of its full significance — the pain is sweet and yet she wants to weep, a verb that conveys both emotional joy and sadness. The immensity of the sensation is couched in the terms of filling — 'full', 'overflowing', 'brimming over' — that imply a continuous replenishment; this current is abruptly interrupted by the punctual flash of thought that conjures up Dadda, a telling echo of the fatal instant of death. While Laura's knowledge of the world increases when she is forced to confront the physical reality of death, Celia's moment of truth is at once more intellectual and emotional. To a certain extent she has been forewarned of the coming disaster at home. When the news is announced the younger children rush to the protection of their mother's arms; Celia does not herself move but her thoughts shift back to recollect that isolated moment in the afternoon. Noticing the basket of fruit delivered from the Big House, she is reminded of the wonderful day — she has already accepted her father's death emotionally and yet remains momentarily too frightened to know it in its terrible physical reality. The basket of fruit acts as a catalyzer which encourages her to communicate; going into her parents' bedroom, she is able to tell her dead father everything about the garden party. Dadda participates in the joy of the day from beyond. Death is viewed in a dreamlike way, but it is a dream where relationship and communication continue; in spite of the smoky lamp Dadda is glowing, unchanged and present. Celia tells her father of the lovely garden party experience and thus transcends the break between life and death. With 'the first glowing tear [that] dropped down her cheek like a golden sun' Celia radiates with the same inner light that distinguished her father during his lifetime.

***

Ihimaera's parallels with and shifts from the Mansfield story throw into relief the diversity of life, education and culture as they are perceived and experienced both by himself and by Katherine Mansfield. His depiction of the aristocratic façades of high society contrasts with the warm enjoyment of the simple things of life by the working-class children and thus creates a social and literary interplay between his view of life from 'down below' and Mansfield's story of the Big House garden party. He skilfully slips into those significant open spaces that are characteristic of a Mansfield text. Some critics may regret the completion of such eloquent silences whilst others will recognize that, although seventy years separate the two creations, it is a mark of respect and a sign of durability that a modern Maori writer has been sufficiently concerned and inspired by her writing to create a new story. The result is thus doubly satisfying since the reader can enjoy an independent story and appreciate the new lights and shadows that the parallel texts throw upon each other.

NOTES

1. I wish to thank Witi Ihimaera for permitting me to quote freely from the typescript of his story 'This Life is Weary', which is to be included in his collection of short stories *Dear Miss Mansfield* to be published by Penguin in 1989.

Selected Bibliography

BIBLIOGRAPHY

KIRKPATRICK, B.J., *A Bibliography of Katherine Mansfield* (Oxford: Clarendon Press, forthcoming).

MEYERS, J., 'Katherine Mansfield: A Bibliography of International Criticism, 1921-1977', *Bulletin of Bibliography*, 34 (April-June 1977), 53-67; continued in 'Katherine Mansfield: A Selected Checklist', *Modern Fiction Studies*, 24 (Autumn 1978), 475-77.

WATTIE, N., 'A Bibliography of Katherine Manfield References 1970-1984', *Journal of New Zealand Literature*, 3 (1985), 87-120.

See also L. GLAGE's paper in this volume, note 5, p. 46.

WORKS BY KATHERINE MANSFIELD

Collected Stories (London: Constable, 1941).

The Complete Stories of Katherine Mansfield (Auckland: Golden Press, 1974).

Undiscovered Country. The New Zealand Stories of Katherine Mansfield, ed. I.A. Gordon (London: Longman, 1974).

The Collected Short Stories (Harmondsworth: Penguin, 1981).

The Aloe, with Prelude, ed. V. O'Sullivan (Wellington: Port Nicholson Press, 1982; Manchester: Carcanet, 1983).

Katherine Mansfield: Short Stories, ed. C. Tomalin (London: Dent, 1983).

The Stories of Katherine Mansfield, ed. A. Alpers (Auckland, Melbourne, Oxford: O.U.P., 1984).

The Centenary Edition, ed. and intr. C. Hankin (Auckland, London: Century Hutchinson, 1988); 5 vols: *In a German Pension*, *Bliss*, *The Garden Party*, *The Dove's Nest*, *Something Childish*.

See also the *Turnbull Library Record* (March and Nov. 1970, May

1971, May 1972, October 1973, May 1974, May 1979) for first publication of manuscripts edited by M. Scott.

The Letters of Katherine Mansfield, ed. J. Middleton Murry, 2 vol (London: Constable, 1928).

The Scrapbook of Katherine Mansfield, ed. J. Middleton Murry (London: Constable, 1937).

Katherine Mansfield's Letters to John Middleton Murry, 1913-1922, ed. J. Middleton Murry (London: Constable, 1951).

Journal of Katherine Mansfield, ed. J. Middleton Murry (London: Constable, 1954).

The Letters and Journals of Katherine Mansfield: A Selection, ed. C.K. Stead (Harmondsworth: Penguin, 1977).

The Urewera Notebook, ed. I.A. Gordon (Auckland, Melbourne, Oxford: O.U.P., 1978).

The Collected Letters of Katherine Mansfield, ed. V. O'Sullivan and M. Scott (Oxford: Clarendon Press, vol. 1: 1903-1917, 1984; vol 2: 1918-1919, 1987).

The Critical Writings of Katherine Mansfield, ed. C. Hanson (London: Macmillan, 1987).

See also *Adam International Review*, 370-375 (1972-3) for first publication of texts, poems, and letters by Katherine Mansfield, and reminiscences by some of her contemporaries.

Poems (London: Constable, 1923).

Four poems, ed. J. Meyers (London: Elek, 1980).

BIOGRAPHY

ALPERS, A., *Katherine Mansfield. A Biography* (London: Jonathan Cape, 1954).

ALPERS, A., *The Life of Katherine Mansfield* (London: Jonathan Cape, 1980).

BAKER, I., [L. M.], *Katherine Mansfield: The Memories of L.M.* (London: Michael Joseph, 1971).

BODDY, G., *Katherine Mansfield: The Woman and the Writer* (Victoria, Harmondsworth: Penguin, 1988); incl. eleven selected stories.

CARCO, F., *Souvenirs sur Katherine Mansfield* (Paris, Le Divan, 1934).

CARSWELL, J., *Lives and Letters: A.R. Orage, Beatrice Hastings, Katherine Mansfield, John Middleton Murry, S.S. Koteliansky,* 1906-1957. (London: Faber, 1978).

CITATI, P., *Vita breve di Katherine Mansfield* (Milan: Rizzoli, 1980).

DUPUIS, M., *Katherine Mansfield* (Paris: La Manufacture, 1988).

FRIIS, A., *Katherine Mansfield: Life and Stories* (Copenhagen: Einar Munskgaard, 1946).

MANTZ, R., and MURRY, J.M., *The Life of Katherine Mansfield* (London: Constable, 1933).

MEYERS, J., *Katherine Mansfield: A Biography* (London: Hamilton, 1978).

MURRY, J.M., *Katherine Mansfield and Other Literary Portraits* (London: Peter Nevill, 1949).

TOMALIN, C., *Katherine Mansfield. A Secret Life* (London: Viking, 1987).

CRITICISM AND BACKGROUND READING

ALLEN, W., *The Short Story in English* (Oxford: O.U.P., 1981).

BATES, H.E., *The Modern Short Story: A Critical Survey* (London: Thomas Nelson, 1941).

BEACHCROFT, T.O., *The Modest Art: A Survey of the Short Story in English* (Oxford: O.U.P., 1968).

BERKMAN, S., *Katherine Mansfield: A Critical Study* (New Haven: Yale University Press, 1951).

CHATTERJEE, A.C., *The Art of Katherine Mansfield* (New Delhi: S. Chan, 1980).

DOWLING, D., *Katherine Mansfield: her Theory and Practice of Fiction*, unpub. doct. diss. (University of Toronto, 1976).

DALY, S.R., *Katherine Mansfield* (New York: Twayne Publishers, 1965).

FLORA, J.M., *The English Short Story 1880-1945: A Critical History* (New York: Twayne Publishers, 1985).

FULLBROOK, K., *Katherine Mansfield* (Brighton: The Harvester Press, 1986).

GODENNE, R., *La nouvelle française* (Paris: Presses Universitaires de France, 1974).

GORDON, I.A., *Katherine Mansfield* (London: Longmans Green & Co, 1954; rev. ed. 1971).

GURR, A., *Writers in Exile: The Literary Identity of Home in Modern Literature* (Brighton: The Harvester Press, 1981).

HALTER, P., *Katherine Mansfield und die Kurzgeschichte* (Bern: Francke, 1972).

HANKIN, C., *Katherine Mansfield and her Confessional Stories* (London: Macmillan, 1983).

HANKIN, C., ed., *The Letters of John Middleton Murry to Katherine Mansfield* (London: Constable, 1983).

HANSON, C., *Short Stories and Short Fictions, 1880-1980* (London: Macmillan, 1985).

HANSON, C., and GURR, A., *Katherine Mansfield* (New York: St. Martin Press, 1981; London: Macmillan, 1981).

HAYMAN, R., *Literature and Living: A Consideration of Katherine Mansfield and Virginia Woolf* (London: Covent Garden Press, 1972).

HORMANSJI, N., *Katherine Mansfield: An Appraisal* (London: William Collins, 1967).

MAGALANER, M., *The Fiction of Katherine Mansfield* (London: Feffer & Simons, 1971).

MAY, C.E., ed., *Short Story Theories* (Ohio University Press, 1976).

MOORE, J., *Gurdjieff and Mansfield* (London: Routledge & Kegan Paul, 1980).

MORTELIER, C., 'The Genesis and Development of the Katherine Mansfield Legend in France', *AUMLA*, 34 (1970), 252-63.

O'CONNOR, F., *The Lonely Voice: A Study of the Short Story* (London: Macmillan, 1963).

O'SULLIVAN, V., *Katherine Mansfield's New Zealand* (Wellington: Golden Press, 1974; London: Frederick Muller, 1975).

SHOLWATER, E., *A Literature of Their Own: British Women Novelists from Brontë to Lessing* (London: Virago, 1978).

VANNATTA, D., *The English Short Story 1945-1980: A Critical History* (New York: Twayne Publishers, 1985).

WATTIE, N., 'Katherine Mansfield Studies Since 1970' in *The Story Must Be Told*, ed. P.O. Stummer (Würzburg: Königshausen & Neumann, 1986).

WATTIE, N., *Nation und Literatur: Eine Studie zur Bestimmung der nationalen Merkmale literarischer Werke am Beispiel von Katherine Mansfields Kurzgeschichten* (Bonn: Bouvier, 1980).

See also *Modern Fiction Studies* (Katherine Mansfield Special Issue), 24 (Autumn 1978).

Notes on Contributors

Gillian BODDY was born in Rotorua, a town so detested by Katherine Mansfield. She now lives in Wellington where she teaches at Victoria University. She is the author of *Katherine Mansfield: The Woman and the Writer* and with two other women she formed a film company to make a television documentary on the life of Katherine Mansfield. The film, *A Portrait of Katherine Mansfield*, was shown at the Cannes Film Festival and was screened internationally.

Françoise DEFROMONT is Senior Lecturer at the University of Reims; she belongs to the 'Bureau de la Filière d'Etudes Féminines' of Paris 8 where she also teaches. She has written articles and a book on Virginia Woolf. *Vers la maison de Rumière* (Editions des Femmes, 1985), and is preparing another one on Katherine Mansfield. Her main field of research is Women and Writing.

Michel DUPUIS is lecturer in French at the Institut Supèrieur des Langues Vivantes of the University of Liège. His main fields of research are neurolinguistics, literaty psychology and hermeneutics. His publications include *Katherine Mansfield* (La Manufacture, 1988).

Carole Froude DURIX is Senior Lecturer at the Université de Bourgogne, Dijon, France. She is Assistant Editor of *Commonwealth*. She wrote her doctoral thesis on Sylvia Ashton-Warner, the New Zealand novelist and educationist. She has published articles on Maurice Shadbolt, Albert Wendt and the Canadian writer Isabel Huggan.

Kate FULLBROOK studied at the Universities of Wisconsin, London, and Cambridge. She is a Principal Lecturer and Head of Literary Studies at Bristol Polytechnic. Her publications include *Katherine Mansfield* (Harvester, 1986). Her current project, *Free Women: Ethics and Aesthetics in Twentieth-Century Women's Fiction*, will be published by Harvester in 1990.

Anne HOLDEN-RONNING read English Language and Literature at the University of St. Andrews in Scotland. In 1969 she was appointed Lecturer in British literature at the University of Bergen. Her main fields of research are Victorian, Edwardian and early twentieth-century literature, Commonwealth literature and feminist literary criticism.

Liselotte GLAGE is Professor of English Literature at the University of Hannover, West Germany, where she teaches Women's studies. Her main subjects are 19th – and 20th – century English literature and literary theory, as well as the anglophone literatures of West Africa and India.

René GODENNE studied French literature at the University of Liège. He is Lecturer at the University of Paris III. His main field of research is the French short story. He is the author of *La nouvelle française* (Presses Universitaires de France, 1974) and *Bibliographie critique de la nouvelle francophone de 1940 à 1985* (Droz, 1989). He has also published four anthologies of contemporary short stories. He is so fond of the genre that he has altogether stopped reading novels — except for Dickens' *Great Expectations*, which is an ever renewed source of pleasure for him.

Ian A. GORDON is Emeritus Professor of the University of Wellington, New Zealand, where he taught from 1936 to 1974. He is the author of many books on medieval poetry, 18th-century poetry, prose technique (e.g., *The Movement of English Prose*, Longmans, 1966); lexicographer, editor/biographer of John Galt, a Scottish novelist. He is a pioneer in the field of Mansfieldian studies: he has published *Katherine Mansfield* (Longmans, Writers and Their Work series, 1954) and has edited *Undiscovered Country, The New Zealand Stories of Katherine Mansfield* (Longman, 1974) and *The Urewera Notebook* (Oxford University Press, 1978).

Tanya GRENFELL-WILLIAMS teaches courses on women writers for Bristol University Extra-Mural Department and is part-time Lecturer at The College of St Paul and St Mary, Cheltenham, England, where she is currently working on a PhD thesis. Her research area is Women and Modernism, with particular interest in Hilda Doolittle, Katherine Mansfield and Virginia Woolf.

Clare HANSON is Senior Lecturer in Literatures and Cultural Study at The College St Paul and St Mary, Cheltenham, England. Her publications include *Katherine Mansfield* (with Andrew Gurr, Macmillan, 1981), *Short Stories and Short Fictions 1880-1980* (Macmillan, 1985, repr. 1987); she has edited *Re-reading the Short Story* (Macmillan, 1987). She is Contributing Editor to Katherine Mansfield in *The Gender of Modernism*, ed. Bonnie Kine Scott (Indiana University Press, forthcoming); she is currently working on a book on Virginia Woolf.

Andrée-Marie HARMAT is Professor of English Language and Literature at the University of Toulouse-le-Mirail, France. She is the author of *Katherine Mansfied et l'art de la nouvelle* (Thèse de Doctorat d'Etat) and of several articles about the same writer; she has contributed an entry on Katherine Mansfield in the *Dictionnaire universel des littératures* (Presses Universitaires de France, 1989). For several years she has taught and done research work in linguistics and 20th-century literature. She is also interested in music (being a pianist of professional ability) and is currently working on a study of musical parametres in literature.

Paulette MICHEL-MICHOT is Professor of English literature at the University of Liège, editor for Continental Europe of *Studies in Short Fiction* and a member of the 'Centre de Recherche sur la nouvelle de langue anglaise' (Paris III). Her publications include *William Sansom: A Critical Assessment* (Les Belles Lettres, 1971) and articles mainly on 20th-century novelists and short story writers in English.

Claudette SARLET is Maître de Conférences at the University of Liège where she teaches the history of French literature and of modern criticism. Her main areas of research are the narrative modes in the 17th century, the social background and the identity image of the writer in the 17th century, and the history of autobiography. She is the co-editor of *Individualisme et autobiographie en Occident* (Editions de l'Université de Bruxelles, 1983) and the author of many articles on the above subjects published in Belgian, French, German and Italian journals: e.g., 'L'Académie française au temps de Richelieu', *Marche Romane*, 29, 1979; 'Autoportrait et sujet de l'écriture', *Penser le sujet aujourd'hui* (Paris: Méridiens-Klincksieck, 1988); 'Les paradoxes de l'image de l'écrivain au temps du *Cid*', *Romanistische Zeitschrift für Literaturgeschichte*, 1989, forthcoming.

Irène J. J. SIMON is Emeritus Professor of the University of Liège, Belgium, where she taught English and American Literature; in 1980 she received an honorary degree from the University of Stirling and was awarded the Order of the British Empire. She is the author of *Formes du roman anglais de Dickens à Joyce* (Les Belles Lettres, 1949); *Neo-Classical Criticism 1660-1800* (Edward Arnold, 1971); *Three Restoration Divines: Barrow, South, Tillotson. Selected Sermons*, 2 vols (Les Belles Lettres, 1967 & 1976); *La Trilogie de Samuel Beckett* (University of Liège, 'Faculté Ouverte', 1987). She has written many articles and essays, e.g., on T.S. Eliot, Virginia Woolf, George Eliot, Jane Austen, Dryden, Defoe, Pope, Shaftesbury, Dennis, and Reynolds.

Francine TOLRON is Maitre de Conférence at the French University of the Pacific in Nouméa (New Caledonia). As part-time lecturer in English she teaches courses on civilisation, trnanslation and linguistics.She wrote her doctoral dissertation (University of Bordeau, 1987) on 'The Advertising Message in 1980-1983'. She is also interested in Commonwealth studies and has set up a research group, C.O.R.A.I.L., which promotes and coordinates research on literature and civilisation in Oceania.

Nellson WATTIE has spent exactly half his life in New Zealand and half in Europe and the Middle East. He financed his studies in Wellington and Vienna by acting and opera singing and for a time he was a solist in the local opera in Salzburg, Austria. He has taught literature in the universities of Cologne, Frankfurt, Mannheim and Aarhus and gained his doctorate from the University of Wuppertal. At present he trains translators in a college in Cologne. He has published on New Zealand, Australian and German literature. He is the author of *Nation und Literatur: Eine Studie zur Bestimmung der nationalen Merkmale literarischer Werke am Beispiel von Katherine Mansfields Kurzgeschichten* (Bouvier, 1980).